SECRET RYE & AROUND

Terry Philpot

AMBERLEY

About the Author

Terry Philpot has written and edited twenty-one books including *31 London Cemeteries to Visit Before You Die* (2012), *Beside the Seaside: Brighton's Places and Its People* (2015), and *Secret Lewes* (2017). He has contributed twenty-one entries to the *Oxford Dictionary of National Biography*, writes regularly for *The Tablet* and has written for a wide range of publications.

To Mary, occasional reluctant chauffeur but so much more.

First published 2017

Amberley Publishing
The Hill, Stroud
Gloucestershire, GL5 4EP

www.amberley-books.com

Copyright © Terry Philpot, 2017

All the illustrations are the authors, except where acknowledged.

The right of Terry Philpot to be identified as the Author of this work has been asserted in accordance with the Copyright, Designs and Patents Act 1988.

ISBN 978 1 4456 7128 4 (print)
ISBN 978 1 4456 7129 1 (ebook)

British Library Cataloguing in Publication Data.
A catalogue record for this book is available from the British Library.

Origination by Amberley Publishing.
Printed in Great Britain.

Contents

Preface   4

1   The 'Antient' Towns: Rye and Winchelsea   5

2   The Places to Be   12

3   Henry James & Co.: A Literary Circle   24

4   Wrong Side of the Law   30

5   Brought to Book: Writers of Rye   40

6   There's an Art to It   58

7   The World's a Stage   73

8   Keeping the Faith   77

Bibliography   93

Acknowledgements   96

Preface

Rye has long been a thriving town and once enjoyed importance as a port, as did Winchelsea. When two towns and surrounding areas attract a – surprisingly – large number of celebrated people, as well as more obscure but interesting ones, possess some remarkable places, and has witnessed some striking events, a book titled *Secret Rye & Around* may at first seem a curious endeavour.

However, there are always stories behind the stories, just as there are stories behind the walls. I hope that this book offers insights and answers to those hidden stories, which can properly be called secrets, about an area that, on the face of it, appears to wear its history on its sleeve.

A view of Rye from the tower of St Mary's Church. (Paul Lantsbury)

1. The 'Antient' Towns:
Rye and Winchelsea

Of the origins of Rye and Winchelsea little is known, but, as 'Martin et al'. show, by the eleventh century they were two of several small ports created as shipping across the English Channel grew, and by the mid-twelfth century were significant ports. Rye may have been a hundred – a taxation, administrative and judicial area – from 650 to 1066.

Rye and Winchelsea lay within the manor of Rameslie, and were promised by Ethelred the Unready in thanks to the Abbey of Fécamp in Normandy after it gave him shelter when he had fled from the Danes in 1013, returning the next year as king, but when he died in 1016, that promise was kept by his successor, Canute, who had beaten Edmund, Ethelred's son, in battle and married Ethelred's widow, Emma.

A view of St Mary's from the direction of Lamb House. (Paul Lantsbury)

The Edwardian High Street, Rye. (Courtesy of Alan Dickinson)

In 1247 the tide of history turned again when the abbey returned the area to the control of Henry III as a result of a negotiated exchange of land. This was apart from a small inland area, now a village and still known as Rye Foreign (the suffix implying the retention of control by the Abbey), which did not revert to English hands until the Reformation.*

Once back in English hands, Rye and Winchelsea underwent a period of sustained fortification. Baddings (or Baddyngs) Tower may have been part of a royal castle built sometime between 1230 and 1250, during the reign of Henry III, and defended Rye from the French. It was later named after its owner John de Ypres (now part of the Rye Museum). Today, only the Landgate, Ypres Tower and a small section of the original town wall in Cinque Ports Street exists of the fortifications. Sections of the wall appearing elsewhere have been rebuilt.

Whatever prosperity the sea brought, it brought its dangers, too. There were violent storms, especially in 1250 and 1287, the latter cutting off Rye and washing away a shingle bar and destroying the Saxon town of Old Winchelsea on which it was situated. The storm also changed the course of the River Rother from New Romney to enter the sea at Rye Harbour. In 1387 part of the eastern side of the town was destroyed.

*Brentnall says that 'foreign' meant that the place was not under the jurisdiction of the Cinque Ports, which, at that time, may have amounted to the same thing.

Above: The fourteenth-century Landgate, the only survivor of the original gates in Rye's town wall. (Paul Hermans)

Below: An old photograph of Rye from the east. (Courtesy of Alan Dickinson)

Raphael Holinshed, the Tudor scholar, from whose chronicles much of Shakespeare's plays derive, wrote of Winchelsea:

> On the first day of October 1250, the moon, upon her change, appearing exceedingly red and swelled, began to show tokens of the great tempest of wind that followed, which was so huge and mighty, both by land and sea, that the like had not been known and never heard of by men then alive. The sea forced contrary to his natural course, flowed twice without ebbing, yielding a great roaring. The waves fought together such that the mariners could not save their ships where they lay at anchor. Some 300 houses and some churches drowned with the high rising of the water.

Edward I determined that New Winchelsea be built 3 miles to the north-west of its predecessor on 150 acres, with the squared street layout it retains today – and it prospered.

However, Winchelsea had not been immune to human depredation long after the Normans and later the French. After Simon de Montfort died at the Battle of Evesham in 1265, Prince Edward (later Edward I), his victor, fell upon Winchelsea 'and chastised it bloodily', for the ports had sided with de Montfort.

The Cinque Ports date back to Edward the Confessor and the first were Hastings, Romney, Hythe, Dover and Sandwich, later joined by Rye and Winchelsea. In 1278 Edward I established them by royal charter as a means of defence. While there are seven, they are officially the Cinque Ports and Two Ancient (usually Antient) Towns.

The ports were safe havens on the Kent and Sussex coast for ships and their crews. Rye and Winchelsea obtained the special rights and privileges that the charter offered them: they were self-governing, with freedom from taxation and customs duties, had trading concessions, and their own courts.

But while the charter encouraged commerce, prosperity and maritime power, it did not deter frequent attacks by the French – nor even the Spanish in 1350, who were defeated by Edward III and the Black Prince in Rye Bay. In 1377 the French attacked and set light to Rye, looted and stole the bells of St Mary's Church, the roof of which fell in. The next year the men of Rye and Winchelsea struck back, attacked France, set fire to two towns, and recaptured the bells. One was then hung in Watchbell Street, Rye, to warn of any future incursions. (The bell came back to the church in the sixteenth century). Walls were constructed where before there had been earthen banks. But even this did not see the end of French attacks – there was another in 1448.

Raids on Winchelsea began in 1337 when 100 buildings were destroyed by fire. In 1359 3,000 Frenchmen entered the town when the townspeople were attending mass in St Giles' Church where the invaders broke in and slaughtered those present. The lane in which the bodies were laid before burial is commemorated today as Deadman's Lane. The French had also destroyed houses, as they did a year later when they again murdered every man they could find. In 1377 they returned but were repulsed by a force raised by the Abbot of Battle.

The Hundred Years' War had caused devastation in the area and did not end until 1453. In none of this were the Cinque Ports blameless when it came to aggression: in 1242, even before the beginning of the war, they were granted the right to sack the French coast (but not harm churches), with a fifth of any booty going to the king.

Rural Rye in 1851. (Courtesy of Alan Dickinson)

An aerial view of the Church of St Thomas of Canterbury in the centre of Winchelsea. (Barbara van Cleve)

DID YOU KNOW?

A woman in Kent who wanted to stock her garden pond with frogs to obtain *cuisses de grenouille* (frogs' legs) bought a batch of large Hungarian Marsh frogs. This was in 1935 and, despite their location, when some of the frogs escaped within thirty days they colonised all of Romney Marsh and surrounded Winchelsea. They are called 'the laughing frog' because when they breed in the late spring, the males make a distinctive cackling sound.

Elizabeth I visited Rye in 1573, entertained, it is said, in Grene Hall, Church Square, and called it 'Rye Royal' in thanks for the reception she received, while she dubbed Winchelsea 'Little London'. But less than a century later the diarist John Evelyn, writing in 1660, found Winchelsea in 'forlorn ruins'.

In the Napoleonic period the area again appeared to be threatened by the French, occasioning the building of the Royal Military Canal, while the pepper pot-like Martello Towers were constructed along the coast.

In the Second World War Winchelsea became a garrison (as it had been in 1794) and in 1942 and 1943 was twice bombed and strafed by German aircraft. Henry James' beloved Garden Room at Lamb House in Rye was destroyed by a direct hit in 1940.

When the sea retreated 2 miles out Rye became an inland town (as did Winchelsea for the same reason). The once thriving ports, which had seen the marauding French,

The ruins of Greyfriars, one of the monastic foundations of Winchelsea. (Michael Coppins)

Rye was not immune from wartime bombing, as happened on the Strand on 22 September 1942. (Courtesy of Alan Dickinson)

enriched England's economy, and gave smugglers a means to a livelihood, are long gone, though Rye retains a fishing fleet.

Tourism and yachting, not the wines of France or imports from further shores or the exporting of England's goods, are today's staples of the Rye economy. A visitor will admire a town that Henry James would recognise in a way that London might bewilder him. But that visitor, too, may not know that where he or she now sees sheep grazing that this was once where the sea once ebbed and flowed. And also that what has shaped Rye and Winchelsea is that sea and the trade, legal and illegal, and invasion and the fear of it, together with the sturdy independence of their people, and the influx of outsiders, be they refugees, like the Huguenots, or the artists and writers and so many others.

DID YOU KNOW?

The mayor of Rye has, uniquely, two pairs of maces. In 1507 and 1562 new maces were made of iron and those used today may well be the originals, having been re-silvered. The Georgian maces date from 1767 and are silver gilt. When the king's bailiff governed the town with the mayor, each had a mace. When the Corporation took over the two roles, the new mayor was entitled to a mace, but also one for being ex-officio bailiff. Exact replicas of the Georgian maces are carried and displayed in the Canadian Parliament.

2. The Places to Be

The Sunken Forest

The Romney Marsh has a forest but one that can only be seen in the sand at low tide. The sunken forest of Pett is believed to be 6,000 years old and is a reminder of when sea levels were about 100 feet lower than today.

It is possible that when sea levels rose and flooded the woodland, they preserved the forest and now, when the tide retreats, its spongy tree roots and branches can be seen between rock and sand, with barnacles and mussels. Here are oak and birch. Hazel nuts, carbon dated to 5200 BC, have been collected.

It is not, however, a petrified forest, as is sometimes said – age has not yet allowed it to turn to stone. Indeed, the trees are soft and breakable.

The Hospital of St John, Winchelsea

The prominent corner of the gable end of an old house, prominently to be seen where the Hastings Road at Winchelsea turns downhill in the direction of Icklesham, is all that remains today of St John's Hospital, probably the most important of the three hospitals once found in the town. At the time of Edward I it was receiving 31s 6d in rents, a considerable sum. 10 acres of land were granted to it in 1586. It was controlled by the mayor, who was obliged to

The remains of St John's Hospital, Winchelsea. (Courtesy of Andrew Bowden under Creative Commons 2.0)

make an annual visit and could have evicted any inmate he thought undesirable, and, with the jurats (the men who, with the mayor, formed a council to run the town), could admit any poor man or woman 'in good love and fame all their time, and have neither chattels nor goods whereof to live, the said man or woman shall be sent into the said hospital, to take sustenance of the said brethren and sisters, without paying anything to the said hospital.'

DID YOU KNOW?
One of the most not very obvious names for a house is The House Opposite at Nos 5–6, Mermaid Street. That's how the handsome Grade II-listed building was named in the early sixteenth century but the question remains: opposite what?

Winchelsea Cellars
The pleasant, ordered streets of Winchelsea contain an unusual feature rivalled only in Norwich and Southampton. For after these cities, Winchelsea has more medieval cellars than anywhere else in England. There are fifty-six; thirty-three of which are accessible, and built in the thirteenth century to serve the wine trade with Gascony (there are also some of a later date).

A cellar at Salutation Cottages, Winchelsea. (Terry Philpot)

They were built before the houses that now stand above them because putting them in after building the house would have been impossible. This means that they are likely to have been the first constructions in the town.

Not all householders owned the cellars below their homes and some were rented. Delivery of goods was made by an entrance in the road, although some deliveries were possible from within the house.

Some cellars are more elaborate than others, with natural light and quadripartite vaulting or Gothic arches, and one has a chimney. They may have been showrooms as well as places to store goods. Thus, merchants could show samples and meet those seeking their wares, like a car or furniture salesperson today. In the fourteenth century the town was one of the main places where wine was imported into England and the cellars secured valuable wine, which was open to theft if kept at quaysides. The wine merchants of Gascony, who came frequently to Winchelsea, would often entertain in the cellars. During the Hundred Years' War the silting up of the harbour and the Black Death caused trade in Winchelsea to decline and the use of the cellars fell away, but never ceased.

DID YOU KNOW?

The Watch House at Rye Harbour, now an elegant private home, is a Grade II-listed former watchtower. It was built by the Royal Navy in 1835 so that ships could be observed as they entered and left the harbour. The house was also once used as a jail for smugglers and drunken sailors. The outside is painted in thick black tar to waterproof it – much like the undersides of ships.

The Austin Friars Chapel

Situated on Conduit Hill, the only part remaining intact is the friary chapel, known as the Monastery, which is a Grade II-listed two-storey building. It is scheduled as an Ancient Monument by Historic England and, owing to its poor condition, it is also on Historic England's 'Heritage at Risk' register. The friars founded their monastery on 2 acres at the east cliff in 1364. In around 1380, being threatened by the sea, which later destroyed the land, and suffering under the French in 1377, the monks settled at a new site called La Haltone.

The buildings and lands were sequestrated in 1538 at the Dissolution of the Monasteries and the friar and a priest were ordered to be detained by the mayor for defaming the king.

In 1645 Thomas Goodwyn paid £1,112 2s 6d for the friary and its contents and a year later it was owned by Anthony Norton, a local landowner. In 1711 his relative, Ralph Norton, owned the property, by now consisting only of the chapel, as well as Whitefriars, which was opposite. It served as a malthouse, barracks, wool store, hospital and cheese and butter warehouse. By the late nineteenth century the Salvation Army had used it as a store and it then became an antiques shop. It was extensively altered and opened in 1905. It was used for local events, and for film screenings in the Second World War, when

Above: The chapel was used as a hospital
for soldiers during the First World War.
(Courtesy of Alan Dickinson)

Right: The Austin Friars Chapel, Conduit
Street, Rye. (Paul Lantsbury)

the cinema was bombed. After the war it became the Cinque Ports Pottery. At the time of writing, it is shuttered, empty and sadly neglected.

Jeake's House

What is now an elegant hotel belies the original purposes of Jeake's House.

The wool merchant Samuel Jeake, son of the father of the same name, was also an astrologer. When he was twenty-nine, his astrological calculations led him to marry thirteen-and-a-half-year-old Elizabeth Hartshorne, daughter of the headmaster of Rye School. Her dowry included a three-gabled sixteenth-century building on Mermaid Street, now Hartshorn House. Consulting the stars, Jeake decided to build a wool storehouse across the road, which is now Jeake's House.

In 1924 the American poet, novelist, critic and Pulitzer Prize-winner Conrad Aiken bought Jeake's House, where his novelist daughter, Joan, was born. Here he was visited by friends, including fellow American poet T. S. Eliot and the novelist Malcolm Lowry, and Rye residents, like the novelists Radclyffe Hall and E. F. Benson, and the painter Paul Nash.

Aiken called his study on the first floor his 'deeply cherished home', which overlooked 'a mile of green Romney Marsh and the blue edge of the channel'. Aiken wrote of the house: 'By how many noble or beautiful or delightful spirits had it been lighted and blessed! Lighted by love, lighted by laughter, the kind of light that never goes out.'

Below left: Now a hotel, Jeake's House was built as wool store by Samuel Jeake Jr. (Terry Philpot)

Below right: The House with the Seat.

Royal Military Canal

The Royal Military Canal is nearly 30 miles long but is no longer navigable by shipping. As a place for walking and wildlife, it seems to blend with the Romney Marsh, but its original purpose is often forgotten. The wild and desolate beauty of the Romney Marsh had one great disadvantage: the low-lying coast lent itself to invasion.

This was never more apparent than when Napoleon set his sights on England. When the original notion that the Marsh could be quickly flooded and would be impassable proved false, it was decided to build a 19-mile-long canal from Seabrook, near Folkestone, to the River Rother near Rye. Water from the sea and the Rother would serve the nearly 10-feet-deep canal.

Troops would be shielded by a parapet built from excavated soil on the northern bank. John Rennie, the engineer responsible for Southwark, London and Waterloo Bridges, was engaged. But the canal would be longer than originally intended – of its 28 miles, more than 22 miles had to be dug. The cost would be £200,000, with completion scheduled for June 1805.

Landowners were won over by the Prime Minister, William Pitt, who met them in Dymchurch and told them that the canal was not only a defensive structure but would assist them with drainage. It became known as 'Mr Pitt's Ditch'.

However, hopes for a June completion were thwarted by winter weather, flooding, and a problem in recruiting workmen. By May, as work stopped, only 6 miles had been completed. The contractors, whom Rennie had blamed for greed and poor supervision, were sacked by order of Pitt – and so was Rennie.

Navvies dug the canal, which was then lined with clay, and soldiers built the ramparts and laid turf on the banks. Hand pumps, later replaced by steam-driven ones, had to be used because flooding filled the trench and stayed progress. But by August 1806 the canal was open from Seabrook to the River Rother, although for most of its length it was only half the width envisaged. Completed in April 1809, the construction of Iden Lock in September the previous year effectively made the marsh an island.

With the English Channel and the seventy-four Martello Towers strung along the coast up to East Anglia, the canal formed a third line of defence. However, four years before the canal was finished, the Battle of Trafalgar ended Napoleonic ambition.

The canal had cost £234,310 and now had no obvious purpose. In an attempt to recoup at least some of the money, it was opened for navigation and tolls were collected to transport goods; it was then opened to the public with tolls collected for the use of the military road between Iden, Rye and Winchelsea. A four-hour regular barge service ran from Rye to Hythe.

However, the canal was never well used and even less so when, in 1851, the rail line from Ashford to Hastings opened. Maintenance costs were also high, so in the 1860s

Camber Castle. (Courtesy of Tom Lee under Creative Commons 2.0)

the canal was leased to the Lords of the Level (the historic governors of the Marsh) for 999 years at an annual rent of 1s for the part that ran from Iden Lock to West Hythe. The last toll was collected at Iden Lock on 15 December 1909.

History all but repeated itself when, in 1935, with war clouds looming in Europe, the War Department requisitioned the canal. Pillboxes were constructed on the banks but were never needed as, once again, there was no invasion.

But as the canal acted as a sink for the network of ditches that criss-cross the Marsh, the area has been improved. When rainfall is low and water is needed for irrigation, it is pumped from the canal into the drainage ditches. When there is a risk of flooding, water can be taken from the ditches into the canal and the excess water let out of the canal at Iden Lock or the sluice at Seabrook.

The canal is the third longest defensive structure ever built in the British Isles, after Hadrian's Wall and Offa's Dyke, and parts are designated as a Site of Special Scientific Interest. The rest is a Local Wildlife Site, and the whole canal is a Scheduled Ancient Monument.

Right: The Royal Military Canal today. (Alex Wolfson)

Below: The Winchelsea Road tollgate, shown in the 1890s, was for a new route built by the military in conjunction with the Royal Military Canal and completed in 1808. This is at the junction with Rye Harbour Road. (Courtesy of Hastings Museum)

Rye, Winchelsea and District Memorial Hospital

Although the present hospital was built in 1994, a hospital has stood on this site since the twelfth century.

The leper hospital of St Bartholomew was built in 1189 by monks who came to England in the wake of the Norman Conquest to revitalise the English Church, and was important enough to be virtually self-governing between 1189 and 1219.

The wars between England and France in the thirteenth and fourteenth centuries caused the ownership of the hospital to switch back and forth depending on which French or English monarch was in the ascendant.

Victory at Agincourt in 1415 by Henry V secured English control of the hospital and surrounding lands but by around 1435 the building was in ruins. In 1660, when Charles II returned from exile in France and reclaimed the throne, his horses were quartered on the Barrack Field, within the area of the old medieval foundation.

The government took control of the land from 1779 to 1818, using it as a military base. Tented encampments now stood on the site where the monks had once ministered to the sick and the poor.

What was known as the Barracks Hospital, to serve the troops, was built in around 1788–9 on a new part of the site. This was demolished in around 1818, leaving only a cottage.

In 1844, a workhouse for 436 inmates was constructed further down the hill but still within the area of the medieval hospital. This became a hospital for mentally and physically disabled people after the Second World War and stood until 1988, while what had been the nurses' home was converted into housing, which remains on the site.

In 1921 the Rye, Winchelsea and District Memorial Hospital, designed by Sir Reginald Blomfield, was opened as a general hospital within the site of the monastic hospital. The present hospital was built onto the back and to the side of the front wall, the only part not demolished in 1994.

Demolition offered more than the creation of a new hospital. An archaeological dig uncovered thirteenth- and fourteenth-century coins and pottery, along with military artefacts, including an officer's wig curlers, spurs and children's toy cannons.

DID YOU KNOW?

Although the exact spot cannot now be seen, a few yards from the road to the left of the Monkbretton Bridge once stood the terminus of a railway that linked Rye with the golf links and eventually went as far as Camber Sands. Two coaches were originally hauled by a steam locomotive known as the Rye & Camber Tram. It was a single-track railway in use up to 1939 and travelled around 10 mph. The writer Malcolm Saville remembered taking it as a boy from Rye 'to the delectable sand dunes of Camber'.

Lamb House

Lamb House has become a literary shrine due its most famous residents – including the American novelist and anglophile Henry James – that this striking, if modest, Georgian house is, at the very least, lacking identity apart from its literary associations.

Lamb House was built between 1722 and 1774* on the site of a brewery and other accommodation for James Lamb, who was thirteen times mayor of Rye, a post held

The Revd George Augustus Lamb
was the last of this distinguished
local family to own Lamb House.

multiple times by subsequent members of his family including his son, Thomas (who was twenty times mayor). James had become deputy controller of customs in 1713.

The first well-known visitor was George I, who came here in 1726, when, returning from his native Hanover, his ship ran ashore in a storm in the Rye estuary. Lamb escorted the king to his home and offered him a bed. Lamb's wife was heavily pregnant and actually gave birth to their son in the night. They named him George.

The king spoke no English and Lamb no German, but he stayed for four nights. The royal visitor presented the couple with a silver bowl and 100 guineas as a christening present for the child, and also agreed to be his godfather.

Information differs about the date when Lamb House was built. Building began in 1722 and probably finished the next year but certainly by 1724, when the window tax was being paid. However, other sources are more definite as to completion: 1720 (Seymour), and 1723 (Montgomery Hyde, Edel, and Channer); while Greeves, in her official National Trust book, says that the house was completed in 1724, although the National Trust website puts it at 1722. Deblanco, maybe wisely, doesn't say.

James Lamb's descendant, Revd George Augustus Lamb, rector for fifty-eight years in Iden and East Guldeford, sold the house in 1860 to a banker, Francis Bellingham, whose son leased it to the author Henry James. James' nephew, also Henry, inherited the house and his widow Dorothea gave it to the National Trust in 1950. Although much of the contents, including almost all of James' library of around 2,000 volumes, were acquired or sold after his death by relatives, some items associated with James, including a collection of his books, have been acquired.

When the BBC used Lamb House to film the Mapp and Lucia novels, by another past tenant E. F. Benson, a temporary replica of the Garden Room, destroyed by a direct hit from a German bomber in 1940, was created.

Other tenants included Benson's brother, A. C. Benson, an essayist, author and poet; the novelist Rumer Godden; the writer, MP and lawyer H. Montgomery Hyde, and the MP and painter Brian Batsford. When Sir William Mabane, the Liberal MP for Huddersfield West and minister, was raised to the peerage in 1992, he took as his title Baron Mabane of Rye, acknowledging his tenancy of Lamb House.

Lamb House, a literary shrine. (Paul Lantsbury)

DID YOU KNOW?

By the fence on the west side of St George's Church, Brede, stands a small oak cross with the inscription 'Damaris'. Next to it lies (buried) Damaris Richardson (1834–56), a poor orphan girl who lived in a cottage in Rectory Lane with her uncle, and who worked in the rectory and a small residential school. She fell in love with Lewis Smith, a local young man living with his wealthy parents in Church House, and the cross marks their trysting place. When the couple became unofficially engaged, the marriage was forbidden by his parents, who threatened to cut Lewis out of their will. He conceded and Damaris is said to have died of a broken heart. Lewis lived alone in his family's home and died, unmarried, aged sixty-five in 1896.

The cross at Damaris's grave that marks the trysting place. (Claudia Booman)

3. Henry James & Co.: A Literary Circle

Henry James looks down from his seventieth birthday portrait by John Singer Sargent: unsmiling, detached, aloof – he appears almost Olympian. One of the most famous portraits of any author, this suggests a certain image of its subject quite at variance with the very human and complex person that he was, and most certainly in the eighteen years that he lived in Rye.

He had visited England from his native America several times but in 1876, aged thirty-three, he came for good. He travelled widely in the next forty years until his death – but he never lived permanently elsewhere.

He first came to Rye as a tenant of the architect Sir Reginald Blomfield, in his house Point Hill at Playden. 'I enjoy every hour,' he wrote. James, a man of famous bulk and quite alien to strenuous exercise, nevertheless often used to go out cycling. He would also take the train to Hastings in the afternoon and walk up and down the promenade.

Never without London accommodation, James took a twenty-one-year lease for £70 a year on Lamb House ('a small, charming, cheap old house') and moved in June 1898. In 1899 he purchased it for £2,000, along with a studio in Watchbell Street. Rye was to offer him 'a long-assuaged desire for calm and retreat' after the dispiritingly poor reception

John Singer Sargent's portrait of the novelist Henry James, on display in the National Portrait Gallery, London.

on the first night of his play *Guy Domville*, when he was jeered and booed in front of his friends.

In Lamb House he wrote, among other works, *The Golden Bowl*, *The Ambassadors* and *The Wings of a Dove*, as well as extensively revising most of his oeuvre. He worked in the Garden Room (built in 1743) in the summer and in the Green Room in the winter, dictating his work to his three secretaries, the last of whom, Theodora Bosanquet ('my amanuensis') stayed with him until the end. One brick, he averred of Lamb House, was worth 'the whole bristling state of Connecticut'.

E. F. Benson, who first came as James' guest in 1900, reported on James' voice, 'booming and pausing and booming again, as he moved up and down the book-lined [Garden] room dictating the novel on which he was at work to his typist'. James had his dogs and four servants – two of whom he had to sack for drunkenness – and a gardener (at 22*s* a week).

Many famous visitors came to visit, among them his fellow American novelists Edith Wharton and Sarah Orne Jewett, the critic and essayist Edmund Gosse, James' brother, the philosopher William James, the novelists George Gissing and Hugh Walpole, and the cartoonist Max Beerbohm. He would meet them at Rye station and they would walk ahead as Burgess Noakes, James' manservant, trundled along behind with a wheelbarrow carrying the guest's luggage.

There was hardly a celebrated person in London whom James did not know, from prime ministers to artists. Sociable but valuing his privacy, James, who combined impeccable manners with a love of gossip and had what Miranda Seymour calls a 'whimsical malice', enjoyed the everyday life of his adopted town. Children loved him and he them, and he attended flower shows and the golf club (but never played). During the cricket weeks in Rye, James would spend time in the tent talking to the women with his back to the game,

Sir Edmund Gosse, a frequent guest at Lamb House.

which, Blomfield suspected, 'he found too absurd to merit the consideration of serious people'. He gave to local charities, had a young priest billeted with him, and allowed the Watchbell Street studio to be a gathering place for the town's Belgian refugees in the First World War.

He came to spend increasing periods of the year there until ill health and a feeling of isolation caused him to spend more time in London.

A number of other writers were living on the Romney Marsh. When James was living at The Vicarage, Rye, before leasing Lamb House, he was visited by Ford Madox Ford (then Ford Hermann Heuffer), who was staying with his wife Elsie Martindale at her parents' home, Glebe Cottage, in Winchelsea. This was along from The Bungalow (now the Little House), Friars Road, which he and Elsie were later to take. (They later lived in Aldington, Kent.) Later, the Polish-born novelist Joseph Conrad rented Greystones in Friars Road so that he and Ford might continue their literary collaboration, while, with his wife Jessie, also renting Pent Farm in Postling, Kent, from Ford. Stephen Crane, author of *The Red Badge of Courage*, rented nearby Brede Place, Brede, from Moreton Frewen, while H. G. Wells lived in Sandgate in Kent. Indeed, it was James and Gosse who were among Wells' first visitors, who came to see if the young writer was in need of financial assistance (he wasn't).

H. G. Wells, an unlikely would-be collaborator with Henry James.

Glebe Cottage and the Little House on Friars Road, two of Ford Madox Ford's homes in Winchelsea. (Terry Philpot)

The grave of Stephen Crane in Newark, New Jersey. (Tony Fischer)

They were never a group like the Bloomsbury Set, sharing a similar outlook on life and work. The writers visited one another, but rarely, if ever, were all together in one place. Wells called them 'a conspiracy'. Their relationships varied: Ford and Conrad revered James; Wells disliked Conrad's work and thought both Conrad's and James' styles over-elaborate; Wells and Ford fell out; Wells was brutal to James in his 1915 satire *Boon*; while Jessie Conrad thoroughly loathed Ford.

Some of them, however, exchanged ideas, and Ford and Conrad collaborated, while James, improbably, wished to collaborate with Wells, whose refusal, alas, bars us from seeing what the result might have been. When the novelist Violet Hunt (living as Mrs Heuffer) figured in Ford's divorce case (a divorce that probably never happened), James cut her out because of the scandal. Crane and James were both Americans, but their personality and outlook could not have been more different. Crane was lionised at twenty-five, lived in Brede for only fifteen months, and died at the age of twenty-nine in Germany, a death that moved James. Wells far outsold James in his life time, yet James was the most prolific, and now probably outsells the others.

The First World War excited James' patriotism (for Britain), exhilaration, anxiety, and sadness. He visited military hospitals to comfort the wounded (as he had done during the American Civil War), sent food parcels to the troops, and lent his London home to a Rye soldier on leave.

Joseph Conrad.

In 1911 James had written of the 'solitude and confinement … of that contacted corner' in Rye, and, ill and increasingly isolated, in October 1915 he visited 'the dear, little house' for the last time before leaving for London and expert healthcare. Nineteen months before he died he became a British citizen. In December 2016, paralysed by two strokes and occasionally mentally confused, he was awarded the Order of Merit. He died two months later.

Sir Reginald Blomfield wrote that 'in the ordinary affairs of men he was just a kindly, generous innocent'. It is a view that many others – famous and obscure – concurred. Edith Wharton called him 'the jolliest of companions', with talk that possessed 'the quality of fun'. Montgomery Hyde catches James' contradictions well when he says he possessed a 'remarkable mixture of deep reserve and expanding exuberance'.

Sargent's compelling portrait captures an aspect of James' character, John Singer, but it is by no means the complete portrait.

Brede Place in the 1890s, at about the time that the Frewens, parents of Clare Sheridan, bought it and rented it in 1898 to Stephen Crane and his common-law wife Cora Stewart. (Courtesy of Hastings Museum)

4. Wrong Side of the Law

Witchcraft

Accusations of witchcraft, which flourished in sixteenth- and seventeenth-century Britain but had a far longer history, were often based on no more than village gossip or a quarrel between neighbours.

Women (the accused were overwhelmingly women) were often stereotyped as old, haggard and childless widows, which has forever influenced the popular view. Pamphlets and ballads, the main source of news at that time, were largely responsible for propagating this image. However, contrary to myth, young widows with children were often the subject of accusation, as Annabel Gregory has shown through her extensive searches of the popular literature and the proceedings of the trials as exist.

Unjust, cruel and delusionary as it was, to our ancestors witchcraft was a threat, a reality. James VI of Scotland (James I of England in 1603) was so concerned about the perceived problem that he had written a book about it in 1599, *Daemonologie*.

A pamphlet from the seventeenth century.

In the history of witchcraft, Rye is unusual for four reasons. First, because the most famous witchcraft trial in the town – that of Anne Taylor and Susan Swapper – ultimately exonerated the accused. Second, because the lives and character of these women deny the stereotypes through records, which include ample testimony and are extensive (itself unusual). Third, there were twice as many witchcraft accusations in Rye than in the whole of the rest of Sussex, and magistrates tried the cases of eight women and one man between 1561 and 1668. The fourth reason that makes Rye of especial interest is that the mayor and the jurats (twelve men elected to assist the mayor in running the town) sat in judgement because the writ of the king's justices did not run to a Cinque Port. This also accounts for the records being so well preserved.

'Sussex as a whole was not a hotbed of witch accusations', writes the historian Paul Kléber Monod, 'but Rye came close to being one.' The reasons why Rye had a disproportionate number of accusations, according to Monod, are, first, that reformed Protestants were enthusiastic in their pursuit of those accused. The second reason was to do with the Weald, where half the county's total accusations originated, far more than in the downlands of Kent. This may be attributable to upland communities that were more divided and less cohesive, and where neighbourliness was under threat and fears of disorder were common.

Anne Taylor was married to a Kentish gentleman, George Taylor, when, in 1604, her mother, Anne Bennett, the widow of a rich and pious butcher in Rye, rented part of a house to Roger Swapper, a sawyer, and his wife Susan. Bennett and Taylor lived next door to the new tenants. Mrs Bennett and the Taylors were well-to-do and part of Rye society, and the Swappers, while not rich, did not depend on charity.

The two Annes were known locally as healers, curing physical ailments but also dealing with spiritual problems. Thus, when the Swappers fell ill the next year, they consulted them. Susan claimed that when lying in bed she had been visited by four spirits, two men and two women, who wore the clothing of the day but in the 'fairy' colours of green and yellow and had threatened to carry her away. To avoid this, Susan had to get Anne Taylor to dig for treasure in her garden.

The Taylors had recently lost two children and this may be why Anne Taylor said that she, too, had seen such spirits, indeed no less than eighty to 100 of them. Anne thought the treasure belonged to her and agreed to the search. Susan began to leave presents – nosegays, apples, powered beef, and cloth – for the spirits.

The magistrates began to suspect that these goings-on were connected with the death of Thomas Hamon, the mayor, and concern was raised by locals about meddling with spirits.

Anne Taylor and Hamon's widow were not on the best of terms and the latter said: 'If it were no matter if the divell did fetch away his body ... to be an example for others, for she doubted that the divell had his soul already, for that he was an evil liver.'

Claims and accusations proceeded thick and fast: of killing, poisoning, even that Anne Taylor had some hand in the deaths of her children. Two indictments – one naming the death of Hamon – were made against the women and Susan Swapper was found guilty of counselling and feeding the spirits and sentenced to be hung, while Anne Taylor was accused of abetting her. However, Anne avoided a trial by escaping to her husband's family home in Kent. Her trial was postponed until the court next sat.

In her third examination, Susan implied that Anne was intent on harming the local people, for it is recorded that,

> Mres Tayler did then tell her that she said Mres Tayler heard that Mr Maior was taken sick that he should dye of the said sickness for she knewe it well, and that she did knowe and could tell all what was done in Mr Maior's howse and in every howse in Rye yf that she the said Mres Tayler would troble herself about it.

However, the trials were interrupted by Henry Howard, Earl of Northampton, who investigated corruption in the courts. He believed that the mayor and the aldermen, who sat as judges, were personally involved in the accusations against Taylor, which compromised their impartiality. But the trial still went ahead in the summer of 1609 and Anne was acquitted, while Susan was pardoned two years later.

Smuggling

While the Romney Marsh has been described as the birthplace of smuggling in southern England, Rye and Lydd in Kent can lay claim to having been the most robust offspring, twins who seemed at one time invincible to the authorities. Winchelsea enjoyed its share of smuggling; indeed, Thomas Monk, 'a poor fiddler' of Winchelsea, was the last smuggler to be shot by the coastguard in 1838. However, other places not far away, like Hastings, Dungeness and Camber, have an honourable (or dishonourable, depending on your viewpoint) role.

The artist Gustav Doré's view of smugglers in the nineteenth century. (Courtesy of El Bibliomata)

Rye's connection with the illegal trade goes back to at least the thirteenth century, when Edward I passed the first legislation appertaining to customs. A request was made in Rye by the Admiralty in 1357 for evidence to be collected against Simon Portier and other men who had allegedly exported wool, with no duties paid, from the port of Pevensey.

But Rye's real rise to criminal prominence in later centuries was caused partly by the fertile reclaimed land offered fine grazing for hundreds of thousands of sheep. Wool was highly taxed and a poor policing system did little to stop duties being avoided. When wool prices fell in the fifteenth century and the domestic market plummeted, there was a need to find other markets, and ones that avoided taxes and duties were attractive. Economic conditions, too, assisted – money made from smuggling was an escape from poverty, hardship and unemployment.

By the seventeenth century Romney Marsh had become the centre of the illegal trade and Rye was attractive to smugglers because, in the eighteenth century, only a ferry at East Guldeford connected the town to the rest of the Marsh.

In 1660 wool exports were banned and two years later the death penalty was introduced for smuggling.

Some supported the 'owlers', as they were known, in their pursuance of a thriving, if illegal free trade, which brought secondary benefits to shops and inns. But others, especially those whose businesses were adversely affected by smuggling, were outraged at illegal imports.

Not only was smuggling illegal, so too were the methods used by smugglers to hide their identities. For example, it was an offence to wear a bee skep, in which holes for the eyes and mouth had been cut. Wearing a mask or blackening the face was a capital offence.

As smuggling grew, so new ways were created to detect and halt it. Riding officers, stationed along the coast to stop illegal imports of wool, were created in 1700. There were Customs House officers, responsible for legal trade, and excise officers, whose duty was to collect taxes on manufactured goods, later extended to various other imported goods. Each port had a Customs House collector, with a troop of officers. Rye had twenty-eight in 1822.

Today, Rye is a town replete with sites of this criminal activity, easily to be seen by wandering the lanes and streets. The two separate half-timbered houses in Market Street, on the corner of Church Square, were formerly the Flushing Inn, as the sign on one attests. It was once used by smugglers. Many buildings, including the Crown Inn on Ferry Road, had a 'tub hole' for storing contraband.

The Old Bell on The Mint, which also had a tub hole, allowed rapid exit by a revolving cupboard that led to the street, a connecting door to an adjoining building, and a series of tunnels leading to the cellars of the nearby Mermaid Inn. The inn also has a concealed door in the bar, which allowed a ready escape from the bedrooms above, now named Dr Syn's Bedchamber and the Elizabethan Bedchamber.

The Mermaid Inn's greatest stake in the history of smuggling is that it was used by the Hawkhurst Gang, who drank there with their cocked pistols resting on the tables. Their notoriety intimidated those who were outraged by their behaviour. When they drank at the Red Lion, they fired their pistols into the ceiling to intimidate the more peaceful clients.

The Mermaid Inn (above) was the haunt of the notorious Hawkhurst Gang, while two houses now comprise what was the Flushing Inn (left). (Paul Lantsbury)

The Old Bell, The Mint, Rye. (Gary Knight)

The gang had been founded in 1735 and made itself felt from as far as Dorset to Kent. In the early 1740s Jeremiah Curtis became one of its most brutal members. Another member, George Chapman, was later executed and gibbeted in his home village of nearby Hurst Green after a battle with riding officers.

It was the Goudhurst Militia (founded by local people in that Kent village, who were repelled by the brutality of the gang) who finally brought the gang to book in 1747. In 1748 and 1749, two of the gang's leaders, Arthur Gray and Thomas Kingsmill, were executed, along with others.

The Mermaid Inn also enjoyed the patronage of a Mayfield man, Gabriel Tomkins, a former smuggler so reformed that he was employed as a bailiff to the sheriff of Sussex, in which capacity he arrested Thomas Moore, a local smuggler, when staying in Rye in 1735.

Bailed by the magistrate, Moore came back to the inn seeking revenge. The landlord, who seemed to know which side his bread was buttered on, helped Moore break into Tomkins' room, drag him through the town and to a boat, intending to sail to France and abandon the bailiff there. But the officers for the revenue searched the vessels and Tomkins escaped.

The National Coastguard Service was founded in 1809 and became a disciplined, uniformed and effective body patrolling the coast and sea. At regular points along the coast there were coastguard cottages to house members of the service, who were crucial in the defeat of smuggling.

Smuggling declined thanks to a great reduction in, and abolition of, most duties as part of the growth of free trade in the first half of the nineteenth century. The customs service, too, was reformed in 1853 and continues today as HM Coastguard.

DID YOU KNOW?
Smugglers' tunnels are said to link St George's Church, Ivychurch, with the Bell Inn
public house next door. It is claimed that some services could not be held when
contraband was stored in the aisles and the pulpit.

Murder by Mistake

Rye's most infamous crime resulted from a seeming grudge that went horribly wrong
through an alleged case of mistaken identity. However, on the basis of extensive reading
of contemporary documents the historian Paul Kléber Monod asserts that while the
murderer was a John Breads, there were two men of that name in the town at that time,
and both were butchers and both had appeared before the local court.

There are very few known facts – even about Breads' motivation, which may have
been revenge, political, or, as Monod suggests, likely insanity. What we do know is that
a John Breads murdered Allen Grebell on 17 March 1743 but, as Monod writes, 'It can ...
be said that, judging by contemporary resources, the conventional narrative of the Rye
murder consists of a few facts sprinkled against a very great deal of fiction'. The story

Hanging in the cell where he was incarcerated in
the Ypres Tower is a replica of the gibbet where
John Breads' corpse was left to hang in public
view. (Paul Lantsbury)

was 'fashioned and refashioned ... by a succession of chroniclers', the most egregious embellisher being the local historian Leopold Vidler. Like so many stories where the facts are few, this story has been embellished with the retelling over the centuries, with the townsfolk adding to it, interpreting and reinterpreting it. But this does not mean that there may well be some truths in the case.

The conventional story would seem to offer a motive. In 1737, John Breads Jr, a butcher who became owner of the Flushing Inn in Market Street in 1729, had been fined heavily (£1 1s) by James Lamb, owner of Lamb House, and then the mayor, and jurats for selling customers short weights.

However, as Monod states that there were two John Breads (in fact, there were three, but the third is not relevant here). John Breads Jr was not the murderer, avers Monod. He shows that in November 1730 another John Breads (the two were not related) was fined an unrecorded sum for an unknown offence. It is this John Breads who Monod believes may have been the murderer, but there is no certain evidence of this. The murderer is said to have planned to murder Lamb as revenge for the fines.

Whichever John Breads committed the crime, it happened when Lamb's son, also John, apparently invited his father to a celebratory dinner on board a ship in Rye Harbour, to mark his appointment to the customs service. Breads came to know about the event and hid in St Mary's churchyard to attack the older Lamb as he returned home. However, Lamb was not well and Allen Grebell, the deputy mayor and Lamb's brother-in-law, agreed to stand in for him. Lamb had insisted that Grebell should wear his distinct, red mayoral cloak because of the cold wind and sleet that night.

Lamb and Grebell were of similar build and Breads assumed that Lamb was the lone figure walking through the churchyard late at night when he saw the cloak, and he stabbed the man in the back. Dropping his knife, he ran off with a shout of 'Butchers should kill Lambs!'

It is said that Grebell did not know he had been stabbed and continued his journey home, complained to his manservant that he had been jostled in the churchyard, then sat in a chair in front of the fire.

During the night, Lamb's late wife is alleged to have appeared to him in a dream to warn him that something had befallen her brother. Ignoring this twice, on the third occasion Lamb went to Grebell's house, and was told by the manservant that Grebell had arrived home safely, but when Lamb looked in the bedroom, there was no sign of Grebell. He then found him in the parlour, in his chair. A doctor was called but the victim was declared dead of an internal haemorrhage. The manservant was at first arrested as he had been the last to see Grebell alive but was released when, an hour later, the blood-stained knife with Breads' name carved on the handle was found in the churchyard. The butcher was charged with the murder.

Monod suggests that the red cloak, the unnoticed wound, the ghost and the unrepentant murderer are likely embellishments.

Breads appeared on 25 May in a warehouse in the Strand owned by Lamb, before his intended victim, James Lamb, and three jurats, having been held in chains in the Ypres Tower. He told Lamb: 'I did not mean to kill Mr Grebell. It was you I meant it for and I would murder you now, if I could.'

The Ypres Tower where
John Breads was kept.
(Paul Lantsbury)

He was found guilty and sentenced to be hanged. He was held in irons and under close guard in the Ypres Tower before, on 8 June, taken to be executed outside the Strand Gate. His corpse was encased in a gibbet (an iron cage) and publicly displayed. This public humiliation of his remains was a sign of Breads being cast out from society. It is said that his bones were stolen because they were believed to be a cure for rheumatism.

A tomb slab in the floor of the Clare Chapel, St Mary's, records that Alan Grebell lies below, and that he 'fell by the Cruel Stab of a Sanguinary Butcher on 17th of March 1742 Aged 50.'

Monod believes that Lamb wrote the inscription as a rebuke to his critics, who believed he had denied a fair trial to a man who was mentally ill, and that he, the intended victim, had sat in judgement and that it would have been fairer for him and the jurats to have Sént the case to the assizes.

Note: Because a different calendar was in use in England at that time, the murder took place on 17 March 1742. The new year then began on Lady Day – 25 March – when it then became 1743.

DID YOU KNOW?

One of the most touching and tragic ghost stories concerns not one but two ghosts. The Augustinian Priory (now the chapel in Conduit Street, Rye) was built in the fourteenth century and sometime after that it is said that Cantator, one of the friars, who was known for his voice and sang in the choir, fell in love with Amanda, a local beauty who lived in the old Tower House, where is it is likely Dormy House now stands on Hilder's Cliff.

She reciprocated and they became lovers but when this came to the attention of the authorities, the couple were buried alive. Amanda was said to be frequently seen, white-robed and white-faced, in the window of her father's house, while Cantator strutted up the lane like a turkey cock, gobbling his old love songs to her. It is also claimed that when excavations took place in 1850, their skeletons were discovered, clasped in each other's arms. At this point they were given a Christian burial and the apparitions have not been seen since.

5. Brought to Book: Writers of Rye

John Fletcher

While we know that John Fletcher, famous for his playwriting collaboration with Francis Beaumont, was born in Rye in 1579, the facts of his local life are obscure. His birthplace was in Lion Street, said to be the site now occupied by Fletcher's House, a tea room. He was the fourth son of Richard Fletcher, who had been town preacher in Rye since 1574 (he later became Dean of Peterborough, when he was witness to the execution of Mary, Queen of Scots, and Bishop of Bristol, Worcester and London). His son, too, may have been destined for a career in the Church.

Though we cannot be sure when or where Fletche and Beaumont met, their three best-known plays performed regularly over 400 years are *Philaster* (their first success), *The Maid's Tragedy*, and *A King and No King*. It is thought that their canon amounts to fifty-five plays, which would also include their solo works, though Beaumont wrote only one.

There is no evidence that Fletcher married and a contemporary posited that he had an emotional attachment to Beaumont, who did marry. Beaumont died in March 1616.

Fletcher went on to other collaborations, with three plays for the King's Company with Shakespeare, though the joint authorship of the best known but rarely performed *Henry VIII* is unacknowledged in the first folio of 1623.

Fletcher died in London on 29 August 1625 and it is claimed (but not proven) that he and Philip Massinger, a later collaborator, share an unmarked grave in what is now Southwark Cathedral.

Richard Barham

Born in 1788, Barham is better known by his nom de plume of Thomas Ingoldsby, under which name he attained lasting fame as the author of *The Ingoldsby Legends* in 1837. These were narratives often deriving from legends and myths of the Romney Marsh, and based on allegedly 'discovered' old documents. They comically and grotesquely mix crime and the supernatural in verse and prose, but they were underwritten by their author's antiquarian learning.

Barham wrote them when a priest in London but from 1817 to 1824, he was vicar of St Dunstan, Snargate, though living in Westhorne. (He became a Minor Canon of St Paul's Cathedral in 1821.) He was ordained in 1813 and gained his first parish in Kent the next year when he also married, a marriage that produced seven children. He died in London in 1845.

An illustration from *The Ingoldsby Legends.*

E. F. Benson

Edward Frederic Benson (popularly known as Fred), son of Edward White Benson, Archbishop of Canterbury, referred to himself as 'uncontrollably prolific', which was no exaggeration for he published ninety-six books – novels, non-fiction, short stories, reminiscences, ghost stories and plays – but today he is remembered for the six Mapp and Lucia novels, four of which are set in Rye (or Tilling as it is renamed in the novels). Mapp, and ultimately Lucia, live in Mallards, as Lamb House is renamed, where the author lived, as well as London. The writer Miranda Seymour says that Benson created 'an Edwardian Cranford'.

Born in 1867 and educated at Cambridge, Benson worked in Athens for the British School of Archaeology and in Egypt for the Society for the Promotion of Hellenic Studies. His first novel, *Dodo*, came out in 1895 to wide acclaim.

Benson was a keen golfer in Rye, represented England at figure skating, and skied in Switzerland, though ill health caused this to be abandoned. He played chess, gardened and went bird-watching on the Marsh, as well as being a gourmet, and a more than passable pianist. 'He was the best company I have ever known', said the historian Sir Steven Runciman.

Benson's older brother Arthur Christopher (A. C.) had been a close friend of Henry James, as had Benson himself, and visited him in Rye, when they had walked through the town and out to the Marsh. Fred also knew Rye, of which he became Mayor, through staying with the society hostess and granddaughter the social reformer of Lord Shaftesbury, Lady Maud Warrender, who lived in nearby Leasam House, Playden.

Benson stayed at Lamb House in the winter of 1916/17 and again the following winter. He and his brother Arthur took a joint lease in 1920, with Benson staying in term time and his brother during university vacations when Benson was in London.

A. C. BENSON, R. H. BENSON, AND E. F. BENSON, 1907

The Benson brothers: A. C., R. H. and the young E. F. in 1907.

Arthur was one of Benson's four remarkable siblings, a poet, essayist, Eton master, and Master of Magdalene College, Cambridge. When he died in 1925, his brother gave a memorial roundel in the south transept window to St Mary's Church, Rye, as he had given the west window for his parents (which shows Benson in his mayoral robes in the bottom right-hand corner). Benson turned down the offer to purchase Lamb House and was sole lessee until he died, the last tenant of the house under the ownership of the James' family before it passed to the National Trust.

Benson wrote a ghost story, *James Lamp*, set in Trench, a very recognisable Rye. The eponymous main character's name may be similar to that of James Lamb, but there the resemblance to the Allen Grebell case ends. Lamp is the caretaker, and his wife the housekeeper of the home of John Storely. His wife goes missing until her reappearance, first as a ghost and, secondly, with her husband, dead in a river, a bullet wound in her head.

Benson was friendly with fellow residents, the novelist Radclyffe Hall and her lover Lady Una Troubridge ('the girls') and each dined in the other's home; he gave them the local tittle-tattle and had them read the manuscripts of his novels (*see* below).

In later life Benson spent an increasing amount of the year in Rye, a place he came to love more than any other and of which he was three times mayor from 1934 to 1937, a post he found he unexpectedly relished. (Lucia also held that office, with Elizabeth Mapp-Flint as mayoress.) He was also Speaker of the Cinque Ports and a magistrate. In 1938 he was made a freeman of the borough. When, in 1935, King George and Queen Mary visited Rye, it was Benson who toured the antique shops with the queen and then took her to Lamb House.

Benson never married and, like James, may have been latently homosexual. He died in London and was buried in Rye Cemetery after a funeral service conducted by the Bishop of Chichester.

The House with Two Front Doors in Mermaid Street. (Terry Philpot)

DID YOU KNOW?

The House with Two Front Doors in Mermaid Street, which dates to 1520, was used in the BBC adaptation of E.F. Benson's Mapp and Lucia novels as the interior of George Pillson's Mallards Cottage. For the exterior, the programme makers went to Lamb House, and in the Channel 4 adaptation Mallards Cottage is No. 29 Watchbell Street.

Conrad Aiken

Conrad Aiken was an American writer, born in Savannah, Georgia, who wrote or edited fifty-one books of fiction, autobiography, literary criticism, and short stories. But he is best known as one of his country's most prolific poets, in which capacity he won the Pulitzer Prize in 1930.

With a private income, in 1921 he and his first wife Jessie MacDonald, a writer, moved to Lookout Cottage, Strand Hill, Winchelsea, and then to Jeake's House, Rye, with their two children, John and Jane. Here their third child, Joan, was born in 1924. All their children became writers. (The marriage was dissolved in 1929 and Aiken married twice more.)

Aiken was mentor to the young aspirant novelist Malcolm Lowry, then only in his twenties, who would stay at Jeake's House. Lowry was much taken with the town, writing to Aiken in 1929: 'I want to be in Rye at twilight and lean *myself* by the wall of the ancient town – myself, like an ancient wall and dust and sky, and the purple dusk, grown old, grown old in heart'.

In 1960 Aiken visited the Lake District home of William Wordsworth with his Rye neighbour and friend the painter Edward Burra. He moved back to Savannah where he died eleven years later, in 1973.

Radclyffe Hall

Born Marguerite but preferring to be known as John, Hall created her own name (as she created her authentic identity as a gay woman) by dropping the hyphen from her doubled-barrelled surname, with which she was born in 1880 in Bournemouth.

Not a town noted for a taste of the outrageous, it is all the more interesting that Hall and her gay partner, Lady Una Troubridge, a sculptor and translator, should have chosen Rye as a place to live in 1930. They moved into their home in the High Street, which Troubridge named the Black Boy, a reference to the swarthy Charles II, who was said to have stayed in it. Hall bought the house, which had once been part of a monastery, for her lover, and while the builders engaged in renovation they rented No. 8 Watchbell Street, conveniently opposite St Anthony of Padua Church, as both women were Catholics.

While sexual relationships between women, unlike those between men, have never been illegal, Hall and Troubridge never hid what they were. Indeed, Hall believed herself to be a man trapped in a woman's body. In *The Well of Loneliness*, a novel about lesbian

Radclyffe Hall.

The Forecastle, Hucksteps Row, Rye, home of Radclyffe Hall and Una Troubridge, called Journey's End when they bought it. (Paul Lantsbury)

The Black Boy, Rye, as Radclyffe Hall liked to call her house in the High Street. (Terry Philpot)

relationships, she refers to gay women as 'inverts'. She cultivated a mannish appearance with short hair, bow ties, monocle, breeches, pipe, and jackets. Some children (and maybe some adults, too) wondered if she were in fact a man.

The couple first came to Rye in 1928 when a friend, Ann Elsner, a travel writer, invited them to spend a weekend with her at her home Journey's End in Hucksteps Row. Hall was taken immediately with the town's cobbled streets, the marshlands, the Tudor buildings, and the distant views of France.

In 1928, *The Well of Loneliness* was published. Hall returned to the couple's London home 'tired but happy', not least, no doubt, because the novel was receiving favourable reviews. She was determined to buy a house in Rye.

By the time Hall and Troubridge came again, staying at the Mermaid Inn, house hunting and taking a lease on Ann Elsner's cottage, a great storm of controversy had erupted and the book's trial for obscenity began. It was banned and copies withdrawn and destroyed. But their new home, said Troubridge, was 'a heavenly haven of peace in which we pulled ourselves together for the next round'. The full force of the law leaned upon Hall and her publishers, and the London house was sold to meet legal bills. In Rye they sought peace, walked by the sea, had tea at the Mermaid Inn, and heard Mass at St Anthony's. The parish priest, Fr Bonaventure M. Scebberas, gave her a gilt medal of the nominal saint and invited her to kiss a relic of the True Cross.

Hall's financial situation was not threatened by the case; indeed, she was independently wealthy. Her other books (*Well* was her fifth novel) increased their sales and *Well* was published abroad. She had spent £3,000 renovating the 'Black Boy', and she bought another place in London and travelled to the capital by Daimler. In gratitude to the church, which was unfinished, she paid for the roof, pews, the Stations of the Cross, and a rood screen (now removed), and paid off its debts. Fr Bonaventura expressed his gratitude by buying her an oak chair for the new house, which, when they moved in, he blessed. On their first Christmas Noel Coward, who lived in Aldington, 17 miles across the Marsh, visited with his lover Jeffrey Amherst, and 'adored' the house, which rang with 'howls of laughter'.

Rye had a gay community that Troubridge and Hall could enjoy. There was E. F. Benson at Lamb House and Edy Craig, whom Hall had known at school, lived in a *ménage a trois* with two female lovers at Smallhythe Place, Kent, which she had inherited from her decidedly straight mother Ellen Terry. But there were many straight friends, too, who were neighbours, like the painter Paul Nash, to whom Hall was distantly related, and the novelist Sheila Kaye-Smith lived in nearby Northiam.

Hall filled her Rye days by writing (the working-class neighbours in Hucksteps Row would feature in *The Sixth Beatitude*), reading, and shopping, especially for marmalade. A ship's bell summoned the servants. When Hall and Troubridge's dog Tulip died in May 1931, he was buried in the garden under a marble headstone.

But all was not always well with the couple for Troubridge had a nasty anti-semitic streak, while Hall could be argumentative, snobbish and was always in the right, but when bested, felt herself hard done by, even martyred. Troubridge had been married (in fact, she was a cousin of Hall's first great love, Mabel Batten, who had died) and had a daughter, Andrea, with whom she had an often querulous relationship, quite capable of firing insults at the young woman. Hall argued with the neighbours, with the servants, and with the curate for his car parking. She petitioned the bishop to remove Fr Bonaventure: she alleged fornication, his confusion at Mass, his temper, his squalor, his failure to minister to the poor, his indecent remarks, and his bad language. She failed. The couple made enemies of their fellow Catholics and Troubridge told them that she and Hall, of superior social status, conceded to have anything to do with them only because of a shared faith. When the church was consecrated in 1933, Hall raged that she had no special invitation, despite her financial support. She and Troubridge had to sit on camp stools to hear the bishop praise Fr Bonaventure.

The window in the Church of St Anthony of Padua, Rye, commemorating Fr Bonaventure M. Scebberas, the parish priest.
(Paul Lantsbury)

Radclyffe Hall plaque on the
'Black Boy'.

The marble pulpit of
St Anthony of Padua.
(Paul Lantsbury)

When the Franciscan Provincial came in November to preach and attacked those who had criticised the priest and advised that they look to their consciences, Hall ostentatiously tore up her seat reservation card, made the sign of the cross, genuflected, and walked out. She sent back the gift of the oak chair.

Hall took against the town – it was dreary, the house a dark and airless prison, infested with mice. The couple bought a flat in London and divided their time between the two places. In 1933 they bought Journey's End (renaming it The Forecastle) for £750 but the Black Boy failed to reach a reserve price of £1,800 at auction.

Even the couple's relationship, which lasted until Hall's death, was troubled. In 1934 Hall fell in love with Russian émigré Evguenia Souline, which led to a long-term affair. Evgenia sometimes stayed at The Forecastle and Hall longed that she should live in her own house in Rye. Troubridge tolerated the infidelity, as she did Hall's other lovers.

Hall lived in the new house for four years, but spent little time there, calling it 'A melancholy little house'. In 1939, she sold it for £1,500 (having asked £1,750). When war was declared the offer was withdrawn, but the couple left Rye, anyway, for Devon, and after that lived abroad and in London.

Hall died in London in 1943. Six years later, with no fuss, *The Well of Loneliness* was back in the bookshops and on library shelves. Troubridge, seven years her junior, survived until 1963.

H. Montgomery Hyde

Born in Belfast in 1907, Harford Montgomery Hyde was a lawyer and an Ulster Unionist MP from 1950 until he lost the support of his local party (and his seat) in North Belfast in 1959, partly because of his support for the abolition of capital punishment and the reform of the laws criminalising homosexuality. After that he spent two years as a professor at the University of the Punjab, Lahore.

He is best known as a prolific author, with fifty-three books ranging from biographies (on Lord Castlereagh, Mrs Beeton, and Catherine the Great, among others) and the law (including books on the trials of Roger Casement, and Christopher Craig and Derek Bentley, and Oscar Wilde).

He lived at Lamb House from 1963 to 1969 and while there, in 1966, he divorced for the second time, and that same year married Rosaline Roberts. At Lamb House, he wrote his biographies of Lord Reading, Lord Burkett and *A History of Pornography*, among several other books.

Hyde was a distant cousin of Henry James and his most relevant work written in Rye was the engaging *Henry James at Home* (1969), which is partly about James' own time in Rye but also his domestic and social life at his homes in London. Hyde also wrote the National Trust's guide *The Story of Lamb House* (1966).

After Hyde left Rye he moved to Tenterden in Kent and died in hospital at Ashford in 1989, writing almost to the end.

Joan Aiken

Joan Aiken was born at Jeake's House, Mermaid Street, on 4 September 1924, the home of her parents: her father was Conrad Aiken, the American Pulitzer Prize-winning poet, and his wife, Jessie McDonald, was also a writer. Her older sister became the writer

Jane Aiken Hodge, while their brother John was also a writer. When their parents divorced in 1929, her mother married the novelist and writer Martin Armstrong.

Aiken was five when she began to write stories. Joan's mother educated her at home until she was twelve, where she learned Latin, Greek, Spanish and German. At twelve she was sent to a girls' school in Oxford. There, aged sixteen, she wrote her first full-length novel and at eighteen her first short story, 'The Dreamer', was accepted for publication.

She mainly wrote children's books – short stories and novels for those age ten to fourteen – but also adult psychological suspense novels.

Before becoming a full-time writer in the early 1960s, she had married, had two children, had worked for the UN Information Office in London, and been a journalist and advertising copywriter.

Night Fall (1969) won the 1972 Mystery Writers of America Edgar Allan Poe Award and *The Whispering Mountain* (1969) won the 1969 *Guardian* children's book prize. In 1999 she was appointed MBE for services to literature.

Her Rye background shows itself very obviously in *The Haunting of Lamb House* (1991) with interlocking ghost stories spanning two centuries, a book that features Henry James and the Benson brothers, E. F. and Arthur, as characters.

In the 1960s she moved to Petworth and, a widow, remarried. She died at her home following a fall in January 2004.

John Christopher

John Christopher was prodigiously productive, penning an average of four novels a year, some under the pseudonyms Peter Nichols (though he was not the playwright of that name), Stanley Winchester, Hilary Ford, William Godfrey, William Vine, Peter Graaf, and Anthony Rye.

He was born Sam Youd in Knowsley and died in 2012 at the age of eighty-nine. He had lived for many years in Guernsey and was well established as a science fiction writer, an adult novelist and children's novelist when he came to live in Rye at New House, East Street, where once had lived the artist Paul Nash.

It was not until 1956 that the success of *The Death of Grass* allowed him to become a full-time writer. As Christopher, he is best known for the Tripods trilogy for young adults, which appeared between 1967 and 1968, depicting a world controlled by aliens from a far planet. The BBC TV series of the trilogy in the mid-1980s was filmed near the author's Rye home.

In 1977 he published *Empty World*, a post-apocalyptic novel for teenagers. In it Neil comes to live in Winchelsea with his grandmother after his family dies in a car accident. However, the town cannot escape a terrible plague that sweeps the world, killing almost everyone, and Neil is faced by fear and loneliness and the need to survive physically.

A fellow writer, Christopher Priest, was a Rye near neighbour and wrote that, '[Christopher] held strong opinions, but was a congenial and pleasant man'. Christopher married twice and had five children by his first marriage, which ended in divorce. At the time of his death in 2012 he was living in Bath.

Mary and Jane Findlater

Born in Edinburgh in 1865 and 1866 respectively, Mary and Jane Findlater were daughters of a Free Church of Scotland minister, although in later life they resiled from dogmatic belief. By the time they came to live Rye in 1923, interest in their books had largely passed, although they retained some loyal readership, and about this time Virginia Woolf and Walter de la Mare wrote to them appreciatively about their work.

Mary published her first book, *Songs & Sonnets,* in 1895 but Jane's novel *The Green Graves of Balgowrie* in 1896 gave them a place in literary and intellectual life. The themes of female independence and marriage as not the only source of happiness open to women were marks their work.

Between 1897 and 1914, Mary published ten novels, two with Jane and two with Jane and two others, while Jane published short stories and four novels. These made them financially assured, and created critical praise and popular esteem in the UK and the USA. Mary was briefly engaged but broke it off as she could not face separation from her sister.

Not finding Devon congenial, they came to Rye where Mary was sufficiently recovered from cancer to supervise the building of their new home, Roundel Gate. They enjoyed meeting people and children, and kept open house on Sundays, when their maid had a day off. 'Feeding the sparrows' was how they described having to put up with tedious people. They were especially interested in local efforts to control the mosquito. They had a series of pet cats that they treated as part of the household. It was to be the happiest time of their lives. 'That perfect time,' wrote a friend to Mary, 'was a jewel in the story of your life.'

In 1940 Jane's heart trouble was increasing and the threat of German invasion with the outbreak of war led them to move back to Comrie in Scotland, a few miles from where they had grown up. Jane died in 1946 and Mary in 1963.

Henry Handel Richardson

Henry Handel Richardson's connection to Rye and its hinterland is as unlikely as that of Henry James and Conrad Aiken, for, as they were Americans, she was an Australian.

She was born Ethel Florence Lindesay in 1870. She and her husband, the Scot John George, first professor of German London University, lived in London and, latterly, Lyme Regis. He died in 1933, a loss from which, her friend Olga Roncoroni said, she never recovered.

The house in Lyme Regis was too small and too remote for permanent residence. Even after disposing of her husband's thousands of books, she still had her own library and two grand pianos when she and Olga looked for somewhere on the south coast, away from the crowds but near enough to be convenient to London.

In 1934 she settled on Green Ridges in Tilekiln Lane, Fairlight, not the largest of houses and reachable only by winding narrow roads 2 miles from the village and where the only neighbouring property was a farmhouse. The house was set high up, with imposing views across green fields to the rooftops of Hastings and Brighton and to Beachey Head. Even a two-storey extension did not solve the problem of the house being too small.

Richardson missed the London circle she had known when she had lived in Regent's Park and would visit London frequently for lunch, to see her friends, for intellectual stimulation, and to visit her hairdresser and dentist, and attend séances in the hope of making contact with George. She enjoyed London for a sense of being 'in things' but

Henry Handel Richardson.

valued returning to the seclusion of Green Ridges, with books to read, letters to write, and walks to make.

Her most famous book, and second of her nine novels, *The Getting of Wisdom*, had been published in 1910 (and was filmed in 1977). At Fairlight, to assuage her loss, she struggled to write and did so in the mornings but her short story collection *The End of Childhood* (1934) and her last novel *Young Cosima* (1939) were not a match her early work.

With the outbreak of war she fed herself largely from her own garden. She could observe the Battle of Britain overhead and living in special defence area, she and other residents were told to prepare for immediate evacuation (as happened in Hastings for three days). The enemy planes, wrote Richardson, 'would drift about in an insolent and leisurely manner', dropping bombs and strafing as they chose.

She and Olga spent half of August 1940 in their shelter, but sometimes, unprepared, sought refuge under hedges or in ditches. Twenty-seven roof tiles were shattered in one machine-gun attack (bullets 'rattled on our roof like hail'). On another occasion a 'terrific' explosion a quarter of a mile away shattered the glass doors and broke windows. Later V1s and V2s were to pass above her house. At one point she moved in land for safety for three weeks and then came back, moving her bed to the hall downstairs, where the staircase protected her head.

None of this stopped Richardson and Olga going weekly to the cinema in Hastings or taking their walks. But food rationing gave her problems as she suffered illnesses, and petrol rationing made travel nigh impossible.

Her unfinished memoir was published as *Myself when Young* in 1948 two years after her death from cancer.

One writer wrote of her: 'Her own view of herself was of a square peg failing to fit into a round hole, but this was a failure that she explored without self-pity. The effect on other people could be daunting, especially since she combined her objectivity with personal shyness.'

Malcolm Saville

Malcolm Saville, the children's writer, was born in Hastings in 1901 and lived largely in London, Sussex and Hertfordshire, until he returned to the local area when he and his wife, Dorothy, moved from Seaford to Chelsea Cottage, Winchelsea in 1971.

Apart from his affection for Sussex and using Rye as a background for many of his books, he also had a family connection with the town. His grandfather, the Revd A. T. Saville, had been a Congregationalist missionary and was minister at Rye from 1878 and oversaw the building of a new Congregational Church on Conduit Hill in 1892. Saville's initials, L.M.S., were a tribute to the London Missionary Society, although the grandson later became a High Church Anglican.

Saville's first children's story *Mystery at Witchend* came out in 1943 (he had published *Amateur Acting and Producing for Beginners* in 1937 under a pseudonym), which was set in a house in Shropshire, near a lone pine tree, and this began the Lone Pine Club series of twenty novels and a short story. Eighty-five of his ninety known books were for children, and he was widely translated in Europe, Scandinavia and North America.

Lone Pine Club books are for older readers but Saville wrote other series for younger children, as well as a spy series, at the time when the James Bond books began to appear. These featured terrorists, anti-Semites, drug dealers, black magic, and the Mafia. There were also books on cookery, the seaside, and two books on the life of Christ.

Chelsea Cottage, Winchelsea, home of
Malcolm Saville. (Terry Philpot)

Almost all his books, including those set abroad, show recognisable places: Sussex, Dartmoor in Devon, Southwold in Suffolk, Yorkshire, and London. His *Gay Dolphin Adventure* and *Rye Royal* are set in Rye and feature the Gay Dolphin Hotel, which is a thinly disguised Hope Anchor, while the former also features a savage storm at Winchelsea Beach. *The Elusive Grasshopper* and *Treasure at Amorys* are also set in the local area.

During his time in Winchelsea he wrote some non-fiction, notably *Portrait of Rye* (1976) and *The Story of Winchelsea Church* (1978).

Some of his books were filmed and there was an early adaptation on commercial television (*The Ambermere Treasure*, 1955–56). He always answered children's letters and enclosed marketing material, setting up a formal Lone Pine Club with a badge and ephemera.

In Winchelsea Saville would plan his writing day by making a daily to-do list. He enjoyed the social side of shopping and in Rye would often go to a pub for lunch. He would go to his eldest son Robin's home, Meryon Court (there were four children), where he would watch the Miss World competition on television and eat gooseberry pie and Battenberg cake, two things forbidden to him at home.

Saville begins his *Portrait of Rye* by saying:

> This book may be described as the consummation of a long love affair. I cannot remember when I first came to Rye, and have lost count of how many times I have returned. Now that I live in her sister 'Ancient Towne' of Winchelsea it is as if I have never left this corner of Sussex where history has been fashioned, and which means so much to those who have discovered it.

In 1981 he and Dorothy moved to Lewes to be nearer their younger daughter Jennifer and her family. Chelsea Cottage went sooner than anticipated and with a home yet to be purchased, they were forced to camp out for a while in the home of daughter Rosemary in Tunbridge Wells, as she was living with her family in the USA. In August 1981 they settled in Ringmer.

Saville died in hospital in Hastings in 1982. Dorothy died in 1987 and the couple's ashes are buried in the garden of remembrance at St Thomas's Church, Winchelsea. As part of the centenary celebrations, the Malcolm Saville Society erected a blue plaque on Chelsea Cottage.

Patric Dickinson

Patric Dickinson had two abiding passions – poetry and golf. This was testified to when, in 1969, he published his autobiography *The Good Minute* with a subtitle *Autobiography of a Poet-Golfer.*

Born in India in 1914, he moved to No. 38 Church Square, Rye, in 1945 when he married his wife, Sheila Shannon. They had a son and a daughter. He became devoted to Rye, a feeling reciprocated by Ryers. Many of his poems are associated with Rye and *Sketches of Rye* and *Poems from Rye* were read at the Rye Festival in 1979. It was to be his home for the rest of his life.

Fifteen years after winning a golf blue at Cambridge in 1935, he wrote *A Round of Golf Courses* about the eighteen best golf courses in Britain, which married description with anecdote and history.

A prep school teacher and BBC poetry producer, Dickinson's Rye years produced *The World I See* (1960), *This Cold Universe* (1964), *More Than Time* (1970), *A Wintering Tree* (1973), *The Bearing Beast* (1976), *Our Living John* (1979), *Poems from Rye* (1979), and *A Rift in Time* (1982).

He disliked visitors whom he encountered in his adoptive town and 'tourists of a sort', and complained of those who 'Through our streets the morons shamble' and 'pile our streets with litter and fag-ends ... Gawping and peering'. Other poems celebrated local matters: 'Henry James and Lamb House', 'A Dialogue Between Church Clock and the Sundial', 'Channel Gale', and 'Camber Castle'.

Much of Dickinson's best poetry came in his later years, when failing health limited other activities. He was a lyrical poet, expressing delight and wonder in the natural world. He also produced translations of Aristophanes and Virgil. He died in 1994.

Rumer Godden

Rumer Godden was another of Lamb House's literary tenants. The daughter of a middle-class shipping manager, she was born in Eastbourne in 1907 but spent her formative years in colonial India, which influenced her writing. She settled in Britain in 1945.

A divorcee, she and her second husband James Haynes-Dixon moved from a Chilterns farmhouse and settled in Little Douce Grove, 8 miles from Rye, when he retired from the civil service in 1960, at a time when *The Greengage Summer*, her most famous novel after *Black Narcissus,* was being filmed (six of her novels were to reach the screen and two others were adopted for television). But in 1963, when dining in Rye, the house burned down and only a few possessions, the proofs of a new book, *The Battle of the Villa Florita*, and the dogs and horses were saved.

Hartshorn House, once the home of Rumer Godden. (Jo Turner)

The couple moved to Rye, living in a rented house before moving to Hartshorn House, Mermaid Street, and then took on the tenancy of Lamb House. Part of the agreement was that she had to show visitors around. Did she know Rumer Godden? asked one visitor. 'All too well,' came the reply.

In 1963 *The Battle of the Villa Florita* was published. It became the choice of America's Book of the Month Club, was extracted in *The Readers' Digest*, and serial rights were sold to the *Saturday Evening Post*. Viking paid a $45,000 advance with a first print run of 50,000 copies. Film rights went for $100,000 for a film that starred Maureen O'Hara and Rossano Brazzi. In England it sold 20,000 copies, although reviews were poor.

In 1968 she converted to Catholicism and the next year she published *This House of Brede* about convent life, which was also filmed, although she strongly disagreed with the liberties taken by the film script.

When Godden's husband died in 1973, he left their finances in some disarray, but she still earned well, especially in America. She tried to escape the unhappiness of loss by working all the harder. While she felt unable to continue to live in Lamb House, she wanted to remain in Rye, a wish granted when a house became available in Mermaid Street.

Her children's book *A Kindle of Kittens* (1978) features Rye's rooftops, cats and citizens, the Town Hall, the Mermaid Inn, and Lamb House.

In 1978 Godden moved to be near Jane, one of her two daughters, in Dumfriesshire. She was ninety when she died in 1998 in a nursing home in Dumfriesshire and her ashes were buried next to those of her second husband in Rye.

Viola Bayley

Like Rumer Godden, Bayley's Indian experiences shaped her work, as did her birthplace of Rye. Born in 1911, the daughter of an artist, in Rother Cliff, a house off Rye Hill on the outskirts of the town, she was brought up in Rye.

She was twenty-two when she first went to India to visit an uncle who was a high court judge. There she met Vernon Bayley, an officer in the Indian Police, whom she married in Playden.

They spent a year travelling on the sub-continent, and two of their four children were born there. In the Second World War, Bayley worked as private secretary to the governor's wife in Delhi.

The family returned to Rye in the winter of 1945/46 and she began the restoration of her childhood home. *Storm on the Marsh* was inspired by Rother Cliff and its remoteness, as well as Camber Castle, and she even drew on her own children for characters in the book.

Rye and the house became a fixed point, a place of return in the years of extensive travel – to Paris, Stockholm, the Lebanon, Turkey and Cyprus – when Vernon joined the Foreign Office. Travel offered Bayley material for plays, short stories and books for children. She published two memoirs, *Early Years* and *Memories of India*. Bayley continued to live at Rother Cliff after her husband died in 1966 and a visit to South Africa in the early 1980s produced *Shadows on the Cape*. Later she moved to a home in the centre of the town, on the corner of West Street and Mermaid Street. This was opposite Lamb House, where she worked as a volunteer. She died in 1997.

Monica Edwards

Born in Derbyshire in 1912, Monica Edwards spent much of her teenage years and young adulthood in Rye after her clergyman father, Revd Harry Newton, became vicar in Rye Harbour in 1927. The influence of this was such that fifteen books in one of the two series she wrote were to feature Rye and the marshlands.

She spent her time at the harbour, went out with the fishermen, rode shepherds' ponies, helped at a riding school, and visited Castle Farm, which was destroyed in the Second World War, named after nearby Camber Castle (or Cloudesley Castle in her books).

In 1953 Edwards published *Storm Ahead*, which was based on her experience in 1928 when she walked the shore helping to identify bodies of the crew washed up when the Rye Harbour lifeboat sank.

When she married Bill Edwards, a local fisherman, her father conducted the service at Rye Harbour Church. The couple had two children and lived in Udimore, near Rye, before moving to a derelict farm in a Surrey valley. Edwards learned to milk sheep, but with the need to earn money, she wrote the first of her thirty-five books. *Wish for a Pony* was the first of fifteen that feature the Romney Marsh, Rye Harbour (Westling Harbour), Rye (Dunsford), and Winchelsea (Winklsea).

The stories feature many real-life but pseudonymous characters that the author remembered from her childhood, such as the ferryman Jim Decks and the villainous Hookey Galley. The central character, Tamzin Grey, was, like Edwards, the daughter of an absent-minded vicar, Revd Richard Grey. Her other series, the eleven Punchbowl Farm books, were based on the family farm.

Shipwrecks, smuggling, rescuing oil-covered seabirds, an escaped puma and the supernatural all feature in the books. In 1960 Edwards was voted children's writer of the year, jointly with Captain W. E. Johns, the creator of Biggles. She also wrote for adults and produced two autobiographies.

DID YOU KNOW?

Enid Blyton's *The Famous Five Go Smuggling* may well be set in Rye – at least according to the theories of author Norman Wright. The book, published in 1935, has a hilltop town, called Castaway, surrounded by an ancient wall. Like Rye, it has cobbled streets and shops with diamond-paned windows, passages once used by smugglers, and is surrounded by a marsh sometimes shrouded in mist.

Wright does not say why he regards Castaway as a stand-in for Rye but Blyton's descriptions are such to lend verisimilitude to readers who know the town.

She attributed her loss of readership to television and the way the world was changing. A reprint of nine of her books in the 1980s did not find favour with a new generation of children.

Her husband died in 1990 and Edwards died in 1998, after suffering failing sight for some years that prevented her walking in the valley. The valley was bequeathed to the Woodland Trust.

6. There's an Art to It

Painters have long been a part of Winchelsea and Rye's history. Anthony van Dyck has left some of the earliest views of Rye in the sixteenth century, which are said to have been painted while he waited for a ship to take him to mainland Europe. J. W. M. Turner visited, and in 1866 Daniel Gabriel Rossetti watched a civic procession from a window of the New Inn, Winchelsea. John Everett Millais stayed in the same inn when painting *The Blind Girl* and *The Random Shot*. John Piper's work was influenced by the Romney Marsh and he and his wife Myfanwy, a writer and librettist, rented Rose Cottage in Rye Harbour in the summer of 1931. Other artists have also lived in the area.

J. W. M. Turner, who stayed in Winchelsea and painted in Rye.

The New Inn, Winchelsea, where both Millais and Rossetti stayed. (Terry Philpot)

Sir Reginald Blomfield

The Menin Gate, Ypres, the war cemeteries in France and Belgium, and a war memorial in the churchyard of St Mary's, Rye, together with the town's memorial hospital, would seem to have nothing in common other than the terrible tragedy of the First World War. Yet the architect Sir Reginald Blomfield (he was knighted in 1919) designed all of them.

The war memorial is one that will be familiar to most people – perhaps even more so than with the towering Menin Gate – for it is the Sword of Sacrifice, which Blomfield designed to commemorate those who died in the First World War. Usually of Portland stone or granite and sometimes of a white limestone found in France and Belgium, mounted on the face of the cross is a bronze sword pointed downward, inspired, it is said, by a sword that hung in Blomfield's Rye home. Most Commonwealth grave cemeteries have the cross, many parish and public cemeteries display one, and it can also be found in places as diverse as Japan, Israel, Greece and China.

Blomfield, who was born in Devon in 1856 and came to live in Rye, was already well known as an architect and garden designer before the First World War. He reordered, restored and extended many country houses, including Chequers, the country home of the Prime Minister, and Lady Margaret Hall, Oxford. He completed the Quadrant in Regents Street, London, based on the plans of the architect Norman Shaw, after it had been halted through dispute and Treasury parsimony.

In 1886 Blomfield married Anne, daughter of Henry Burra of Rye, and built them a house in Hampstead in 1892. They were settled there with their three children when one day, playing cricket in Rye, Blomfield saw a cottage, which became Point Hill, perched on

Left: The Cross of Sacrifice, St Mary's Church, Rye. Sir Reginald Blomfield's tribute to the dead of the First World War is to be found in the humblest parish church, as well as Arlington Cemetery, Washington DC. (Paul Lantsbury)

Below: The Menin Gate, Ypres, the greatest of Reginald Blomfield's public monuments. (agracier)

a cliff. There were few views like it anywhere, 'and if the place was to be had, I meant to have it', he said. He bought the cottage, a strip of land below the cliff and a 4-foot right of way for £320. He moved out James Hoad, the tenant of the cottage, who became his gardener and rented the house to Henry James when the family was in London.

Over time he brought up adjacent properties to expand the garden, create a tennis court, and add to the house, so that by 1912 it had nine bedrooms and three bathrooms. 'It is a picturesque jumble of walls, chimneys, gables, hips and dormers,' writes Blomfield's biographer Richard Fellows. There is an observation turret that Blomfield used as a washroom.

He also made other marks on Rye and thereabouts, with his work running to cottages; alterations to Leasam House, Playden; five houses on Point Hill, including his own; houses in Gun Garden and Watchbell Street; Saltcote Place (now a hotel); the Water Tower; the vicarage of St Mary's and its mission room; and the Monastery (the remaining part of the Austin Friars Chapel on Conduit Hill, Rye.

Blomfield was an active citizen. With others, he started the Rye golf links in the 1890s and during Rye Week used to captain the local cricket team. In the First World War he organised a guard for the railway bridge that crossed the Rother just below his house and undertook duties himself. He designed (at no cost) the memorial hospital, which also commemorated the First World War dead; this opened in 1921 and was demolished in 1994. He died at his London home in 1942.

Mabel Lucie Attwell

Mabel Lucie Attwell (she always used her three names professionally) is known more than fifty years after her death for the sentimentalised, rotund, cuddly infants that are still found as dolls and on cards and calendars that she created as an illustrator. She was born in London's East End in 1879, the daughter of a butcher, and educated privately at the Cooper's Company, where an early talent for art showed itself. She started her 'cute' pictures in 1914 and she continued to perfect them when, in the 1920s, she came to live at Robin Hill, Mermaid Street.

She attended art schools but disliked still life drawing, preferring imaginary subjects that were connected with her enjoyment of fairy tales. After her drawings appeared in *The Tatler* and *The Bystander*, her work, at 20 guineas a time, was in quick and steady demand. Until the end of her life commissions came her way. She illustrated *Mother Goose, Alice in Wonderland, Hans Andersen's Fairy Tales, Children's Stories from French Fairy Tales, Grimms' Fairy Tales, Peter Pan,* and an abridged version of *The Water Babies.* Magazine work was a lucrative sideline.

She married in 1908 and had a daughter and two sons, one of whom predeceased her in 1935. When living in Rye she was visited by Beatrix Potter, to which end Robin Hill appears on the dust jacket for Potter's *Tale of the Faithful Dove,* which is set in Rye and Winchelsea.

By the time she was living in Rye, her 'cute' infants were ubiquitous. But Attwell was also influential in how adults reacted to children, not just as dimple-cheeked, chubby kiddies but in how she created, rather than reacted to, new fashions in dress and in the bobbing of hair.

Outside of work and family, Attwell had few interests. She moved to Cornwall, where she died at her home in Fowey in 1964.

Clare Sheridan

Clare Sheridan was born in 1885 in London, one of three children of Clara (one of the three famed American-born Jerome sisters), and Moreton Frewen, son of a wealthy Sussex landowner. Through her aunt Jenny she was cousin to Winston Churchill. Much of her early life was spent at Brede Place, Brede, and she ended her days in Hastings, 8 miles to the south. In between, she established herself as a noted sculptor, with Lenin, Trotsky, Gandhi and her cousin among her subjects, and as a foreign correspondent, while moving from communism to Catholicism.

Brede Place was a near-derelict house on the Frewen estate built, as a great hall attached to an older chapel in 1350. Clara decided she wanted to purchase it from Moreton's brother Edward, along with a couple of hundred acres of park, and make it into a family home. Moreton was known as 'Mortal Ruin' due to a dissolute life, gambling and unwise investments that created periods of threatened bankruptcy, not staved off by Moreton or Clara's inherited wealth, but that was no deterrent to Clara's spending £5,000 on the house. It was almost immediately rented (in 1898) to Stephen Crane and his common-law wife Cora Stewart.

By the time Clare was in her teens, the Frewens were living in Brede Place (but Moreton was often travelling) and here she met the novelists Rudyard Kipling, Henry James (who encouraged her in her literary ambitions) and George Moore (who dissuaded her) and the King and Queen of Romania, among others. She would also cycle to lunch with James at Lamb House in Rye.

She lived at Brede Place until she married Wilfred Sheridan, a descendant of the playwright, in 1910, who was to die at the Battle of Loos in 1915. She would continue to visit Brede Place, and often, too, leave her children Richard (Dick) and Margaret (another

A 1910 painting of Clare Sheridan, communist and Catholic, sculptor and war correspondent.

daughter, Elizabeth, had died in infancy) there in the care of their grandmother as her work as a sculptor developed, which necessitated much travel, as did her work as a foreign correspondent.

When the widowed Clara died in 1935, she bequeathed the house to Sheridan's brother Oswald, who then sold it to Sheridan's son Dick, who installed electric light and proper plumbing and then rented it out. That same year Dick died of peritonitis in Africa. He was twenty-one.

With the coming of war, Sheridan left London for a cottage she built on the estate and Brede Place was requisitioned by the Army. She had the soldiers cut down dead trees. In 1941, from a great oak, she created a Madonna in memory of Dick, which was placed in the Lady Chapel in Brede's medieval Church of St George, where it stands today.

With her son dead, her daughter serving in the forces, the Army occupying Brede Place for a war that she, as a pacifist, did not believe in, Sheridan was lonely in enforced isolation but committed still to her art, although she did stay with her cousin in No. 10 Downing Street to undertake his sitting for a bust. When peace came, she moved back into Brede Place. In 1946 Churchill visited and he and future biographer, the writer Anita Leslie stayed, as did her father, the writer Sir Shane Leslie.

But that year, the memories of Brede, beautiful but desolate, and its financial burdens were too great and Sheridan sold it (it later came into the ownership of her nephew, Roger Frewen), and in 1947 moved to Galway Bay, eventually to her own house, the Spanish Arch, and shipped several bronzes and a number of four-poster beds, as well as tree trunks to carve statues for Irish churches.

Clare Sheridan's Madonna in St George's Church, Brede. (Terry Philpot)

The bust by Clare Sheridan of her cousin Winston Churchill.

She continued to work and travel extensively. She was received into the Catholic Church in Assisi in the 1940s. In 1956 she bought Belmont House, an Italianate villa in High Wickham, near Hastings, converting a turret room into a private chapel. She became as much a character – with her full skirts and silk scarves – in Hastings as she was in Ireland.

When she died in 1970, she was buried in the churchyard at Brede. Seven years after Sheridan was laid to rest, a fire swept through Brede House, destroying the roof, while the chapel remained untouched. Rebuilt in its old style, it is now a private residence.

Paul Nash

In 1929, at forty years of age, Paul Nash faced conflicts, concerns and dilemmas. He and his wife Margaret had been living in Dymchurch, 16 miles from Rye, where he painted some notable seascapes, and then, in 1925, moved to Oxenbridge Cottage, Readers Lane, Iden, 2½ miles from Rye.

His successful exhibition at London's Leicester Galleries the previous year had, nevertheless, indicated to him how easy it would be to 'settle down to a delightful way of painting that would have secured him a very large income in a very short time', as his wife remarked in her memoir. He knew, too, that his father was dying, an event that would be both traumatic and disruptive of family and personal relationships. Also the horrors he

The home of Paul Nash in East Street, Rye. (*Inset*) The plaque to commemorate Paul Nash on his former home. (Both Paul Lantsbury)

had observed in the trenches of the First World War, where, serving as an official war artist, he had been gassed and nearly died, were little more than a decade behind him.

To effect a change the Nashs, with friends Ruth Clark and fellow artist and Ryer Edward Burra, took off for six weeks in Paris, Toulon and the south of France. There he drew scenes in hotels, cafés and the sea shore.

The Nashes returned to Iden but in 1930 bought New House, East Street, Rye, which they moved into in December 1931, partly to give a home to Margaret's widowed father and allow Nash studio space, which he had never had. In Iden and Rye he produced water colours and oils from the journey through France. The café scenes were to influence him ever after. Their large mirrors gave him the idea of the mirror image, which allowed him to depict objects in a room, a motif in his later works *Harbour and Room, Voyagers of the Moon* and *Glass Forest*. His work is characterised by its angularity, diagonal shapes, bleachy tone, and lack of people.

After a visit to the USA in September 1931, Nash and Margaret found problems of maintaining the large Rye house, even though Margaret's father made a contribution, but he died in 1932.

Two exhibitions failed and Nash started work as an art critic for the *Weekend Review* and *The Listener*. His articles about Picasso and de Chirico also show his new interest, originating in that French trip, in surrealism. *Kinetic Feature*, one his most important abstracts, dates from the Rye years. *Rye Marshes* (1932) was used by Shell in its advertising. Nash made money by working on designs for china, glass and textiles.

In the 1930s he began to collect driftwood, bones and stones, using them to create 'object-personages' in landscape composition and may well have done some collecting near Rye.

Early in 1933 Nash became ill with influenza, followed by a serious bout of bronchial asthma, which he had developed in 1929. He was advised that the Rye climate did not suit him. In July 1933 the Nashes moved from Rye, never to return. Paul Nash died in a hotel in a suburb of Bournemouth in 1946, aged fifty-seven.

Brian Cook

Brian Cook, one of the least known of Rye's artists, had a varied life. Born in Buckinghamshire in 1910, in 1946 he took his mother's maiden name to become Brian Batsford at the suggestion of his uncle Harry, who was chairman of the family publishing house of B. T. Batsford.

He was known as Cook for his artistic work and began to paint in 1924 when at Repton, where the headmaster Geoffrey Fisher, later Archbishop of Canterbury, said to him, 'Well, Cook, all I can say is that, if nothing else, you have learned to paint'. In 1928 he began working for the production department of the family firm.

It was here that he developed his instantly recognisable style. Cook's first dust jacket for the firm was for *The Villages of England* (1932). The distinctive vibrant colours were achieved by the Jean Berté process, which used rubber plates and water-based inks. His was a distinctive and attractive style, with characteristic blue trees, mauve shadows, brown streets, bright orange roofs and yellow skies. He worked as a dust jacket designer for the firm, as well as doing poster work for the British Tourist Board in the same style. His work was publicly exhibited, including at London's Hayward Gallery.

He went on to paint many other works in Batsford's 'English Life', 'Villages of England', and 'British Heritage' series, comprising among other subjects English downland, English abbeys, Scottish Highlands, Scottish border country, forestry and woodland, the Cinque Ports, and Bristol, York and Cambridge. Much of his work was done when touring Britain for the company in a Morris Oxford.

Having seen wartime service as Flight Lieutenant Brian Cook, he failed to win Chelmsford for the Conservatives but did serve as an MP again for Ealing South from 1958 to 1974, in which latter year he received a knighthood for political services. He had become a director of the company in 1935 and after his uncle's death, he was chairman of Batsford from 1952 until 1974.

Much of his work is collected in books like *Landscapes of Britain* (2011) and *The Britain of Brian Cook* (1987), which was published the year he gave up the tenancy of Lamb House, which he had taken in 1980. He moved there from No. 10 Watchbell Street. At the time of his death in 1991 he was living at Buckland House, Mill Road, Winchelsea.

His nephew-in-law, Simon Master, wrote of Cook seeing 'Rye across an unspoilt English landscape that his life and work had done so much to celebrate'.

Edward Burra

Although born in London in 1905, Rye was the place where Burra spent all of his life and to which he returned from his travels throughout the UK and Europe and from four visits to the USA. He found his busy social life, frequently spent in London, exhausting, and Rye was the place to recover.

His home was Springfield Lodge, set in large grounds with a beautiful sloping garden, on Rye Hill, Playden, cared for by eight servants. His parents had inherited it from Burra's grandparents. His father Henry, a barrister, JP, and one-time chairman of East Sussex County Council, had been born there, and his mother, Emmentrude, was born in nearby Salehurst. In 1953 maintenance and staff costs forced Burra's now ageing parents to give up the house and move to Chapel House, a red-brick house next to Ypres Tower. Edward went with them.

He was older than his two sisters, one of whom, Betsy, died when she was twelve, and Burra and his sister Anne enjoyed visits to the Rye cinema and trips to the beach at Camber Sands. He attended art classes in Rye and boarded at prep school in Potters Bar, Hertfordshire, but was withdrawn due to ill health. He suffered all his life from a form of anaemia that he may have inherited from his mother, as well as rheumatoid arthritis. This makes his physical and creative energy all the more surprising.

Burra exhibited at the Rye Art Society in 1926 and from 1921 to 1923 he attended Chelsea Polytechnic School of Art, and from then the Royal College of Art until 1925. He had a one-man show at the influential Leicester Galleries, London, in 1929. He had met Paul Nash in 1925. Nash, later to move to Rye, was thirty-six and Burra was twenty, one an established artist, the other unknown. He met the older man 'with the greatest charm', he said, who showed him his engravings and prints. But Burra never took to Nash's promiscuous wife Margaret.

Nash was to play a critical part in encouraging Burra in his artistic ambitions, and it was Nash who, in 1931, introduced Burra to another Rye resident, the American prize-winning poet Conrad Aiken, whom Burra found 'amusing' and with whom he shared an interest in low-life subjects. 'Amusing' was a word that Nash, with whom Burra travelled, also used of the painter: 'an eccentric, talented delicate creature, extremely amusing'.

John Deth (1931) is based on Aiken's poem of the same title and in 1937 they travelled together to Mexico. While Aiken loved Rye in a sentimental way as perhaps an American would, Burra did not, particularly the ancient houses where one 'couldn't walk a step without falling over a dormer window or something'. He found the town 'charmless', calling it 'tinsel town. It was dull and bourgeois'.

Some of his cubist and surrealist work is populated by elongated, exaggerated and large figures. Much of his satire was directed at what he observed on the Italian Rivera, and the nightclubs, dance places and music halls of Paris, which he visited with Nash, and elsewhere. His severely arthritic hands determined that his medium would be watercolours, bold, bright, strong, and distinctive, although there are some oils and collages. In depictions of the seamier clubs and bars visited by sailors in Marseilles and Toulon are echoes of Toulouse-Lautrec and George Grosz, but Burra's is a very English style.

Burra experienced some of the most interesting places of his century. There was Paris in the 1920s and the USA in the 1930s, when he lived in Harlem and painted local life. He arrived in Spain at the outbreak of the Spanish Civil War and his paintings of the conflict are arresting. In the Second World War he lived in Rye but was not immune from events (or from physical pain as he raided chemists' for aspirin). Rye was, after all, a centre for military activity and it looked across to the conquered continent. *Soldiers at Rye* (1941) is a striking piece. He also gardened and looked after the refugees whom his parents took in.

After the war, his art changed and when someone asked him why he no longer painted satirically, he said, 'What can a satirist do after Auschwitz?' Burra's art became darker and, arguably, deeper. He turned to landscapes, often ones of lonely places in Ireland and Yorkshire, but in the same surrealist style and he became increasingly concerned about what he saw as modernity: fossil fuels and road building changing the countryside and a way of life. He also began to design sets for the ballet, opera and a musical play.

Rye, of course, was far removed from the *demi-monde* of Paris or the drama of Spain and may have served as a place for recovery to allow him to paint. Burra's friend Desmond Corcoran, the London gallery owner, wrote, 'I went down to visit him near the end of his life, which was a surreal experience – bottles of gin, cans of food, drawings all over the floor and music playing ... He painted flat on the table, with a glass of gin on one side, and worked out from the centre of the paper.'

He never moved away from Rye, but then moving to his favoured Brighton would have been time-wasting, something he sought to avoid. He called Rye 'Wry', a 'ducky little Tinkerbell towne [that] is like an itsy bitsy morgue, quayte dead ... I come from the land of the living dead'. It was also 'Fort Dung Box'. As he grew older he liked it all the less because by the late 1960s, aided by a large Pontin's holiday camp at Camber Sands, its streets were crowded with visitors. He had never liked crowds and now, often laden with a shopping bag, he was forced to struggle through them. His increasing disability made venturing on to its cobbled and steep streets and narrow pavements a worry should he fall. In 1969 Burra moved to one of the two pleasant gardeners' cottages that he and his sister had inherited from their father as part of the Springfield estate.

Despite how he regarded the town, it exercised an almost gravitational pull until he died in hospital in Hastings on 22 October 1976, where he was cremated.

John Ryan

John Ryan, the creator of Captain Pugwash, spent his early years very differently from his last ones. Born in Edinburgh in 1921, the son of a diplomat, he travelled extensively in Turkey and Morocco before coming back to the UK to be educated at prep school and Ampleforth College, where his first cartoons were published in the school magazine.

By the time he moved to Gun Garden Lodge, Gun Garden, Rye, in 1987, he was an established cartoonist and illustrator. Between those dates he had seen wartime service, studied art at the Regent Street Polytechnic (1946–48), and met Priscilla Ann Blomfield, granddaughter of the celebrated architect Sir Reginald Blomfield, who had lived in Rye. They married at St Mary Moorfields Catholic Church, London, in January 1950, and had three children.

Ryan taught for a while at prep school and at Harrow, during which time he started contributing strips to such children's comics as *Eagle*, *Girl* and *Swift*. He turned to full-time work as a writer, illustrator, animator and cartoonist in 1955.

Captain Horatio Pugwash, the eighteenth-century skipper of *The Black Pig*, 'the bravest, most handsome pirate of the Seven Seas', made his first appearance when *Eagle* appeared in 1950. With his cries of 'Dolloping doubloons!', 'Kipper me capstans!', and 'Coddling catfish!', and his portly figure, dressed in a red and black shirt under a blue frock coat, and wearing a skull and cross bones hat, the cowardly and conceited seaman became a firm favourite.

But the cartoon was unexpectedly dropped by the comic within a few months, to be replaced by Harris Tweed, Extra Special Agent, also penned by Ryan. However, Pugwash was revived in the *Radio Times* from 1960 to 1968, and in 1957 *Captain Pugwash: A Pirate Story* appeared, the first of more than fifty books written and illustrated by Ryan. In their studio in London Ryan and his wife animated the character with fifty-eight 16 mm film, five-minute black and white episodes that were shown on BBC television between 1957 and 1966. There was later a colour series of thirty, five-minute episodes (1974–75) and other animated series of his work, some on commercial television.

Ryan was not easily missed at 6 feet 2 inches tall, with ruddy cheeks and blue eyes, and often walking his dog. Not surprisingly given his work, he was said to have a childlike humour and be delightful company. Locally, he was popular, well known and active, taking part in fundraising for charity, while also designing and painting pantomime sets regularly for the Rye Players. One of his local works was a large nativity scene displayed each year at the Town Hall. The Rye Gallery exhibited his work, as did the Royal Festival Hall, and the Royal Academy summer exhibition. Two of his thirty-seven books, *Murder in the Churchyard* and *Captain Pugwash and the Huge Reward*, are set in Rye. The first is an idiosyncratic retelling, in cartoon format, of the murder of Allen Grebell. In the book Rye becomes Sinkport and while the buildings in the illustrations are immediately recognisable, the streets and buildings have been thinly but amusingly disguised as Barmaid Street, Mutton House, Witchball Street, Baddie's Tower, the Sand Gate, Soap Walk, Least Street, the Gingarden, and the Jolly Jailer.

A devout Catholic, in 1964 Ryan began to illustrate a column in the *Catholic Herald*, and until two years before his death in 2009 he produced weekly topical cartoons for the paper. He created 2,000 drawings, many of which featured the amiable but corrupt Cardinal Grotti in the Vatican. His work for the paper 'kept him in gin', he once said.

He died of cancer at Rye Hospital and was cremated at Hastings, with his ashes buried in the churchyard of St Michael's, Playden. He was survived by Priscilla and their children. A memorial service was held on 5 September at St Mary's.

At the time of his death three successful stage productions about Pugwash had been staged in the UK. He said of the captain:

Pugwash has two qualities which I believe are present in all of us to some degree: cowardice and greed. It is the conflict between these opposing emotions which make the stories work. It may be that the captain is popular because we all have something in common with him. What would YOU do if you saw a delicious toffee on the nose of a crocodile?

The home of John Ryan in Gun Garden, Rye. (Paul Lantsbury)

DID YOU KNOW?

There was a 'pleasant doziness' about Winchelsea said the Pre-Raphaelite Dante Gabriel Rossetti, who came in 1866. Another of the brotherhood was John Everett Millais, who sometimes stayed with William Holman Hunt at Pett. He also stayed in The Glebe in Winchelsea, to which he may have been introduced by his friend, the novelist William Makepeace Thackeray. *The Blind Girl*, with Strand Hill as a background, is a work of 1854 painted by Millais in Winchelsea, along with *The Random Shot*, which features the tombs of St Thomas' Church.

Lucien Pissarro (1863–1944), son of the more famous Camille, came in the summer of 1913 and has many paintings of Rye and thereabouts in the impressionist and neo-impressionist style. He was accompanied by fellow painters Christopher Wood (1901–30) and J. B. Mason (1879–1945), later director of the Tate.

Howard Stormont and Mary Stormont

The artistic couple were married at St Mary's Church, having eloped to Rye in 1898 (he was twelve years her senior). They were visited by artists and Beatrix Potter stayed with them when holidaying in the town. Their lasting contribution is the endowment fund and their home that they left to create what is now the Rye Art Gallery in the High Street, which houses their own permanent collection. It was established after Mary died in 1962, Howard having died in 1935. The gallery is partly formed by combining two houses by a small staircase: the Stormonts' Ypres Studio, their Arts and Crafts home in Ockmans Lane where they had painted, and the home of the artist Eileen Easton, who lived at No. 107 High Street.

Howard and Mary Stormont in the studio of their home, which is now part of the Rye Art Gallery, which they created. (Courtesy of Alan Dickinson)

The grave shared by Howard and Mary Stormont in Rye Cemetery. (Terry Philpot)

7. The World's a Stage

Ellen Terry

At the end of the summer of 1896 Ellen Terry rented Tower Cottage in Winchelsea for herself and her children from her friend Alice Comyns Carr, who would soon work as the designer of her dresses and lived next door with her husband Joseph, the drama critic of the *Pall Mall Gazette*. Terry kept a house in London and her friend Graham Robertson called her new home 'a house built to the ivied wall of the ancient Town [*sic*] Gate'.

Terry was forty-nine when she took the house and well established on the London stage. She had been married twice (divorced from her first husband and separated from her second husband) and had two children, Edward and Edith (Edy) with the architect and designer Edward William Godwin, whom she never married. In 1907 she married for the third time. She was not just a great actress but one adored by the public because of her warmth, liveliness, great spirit and sense of fun.

Her most frequent guest at her home was Sir Henry Irving, himself a great ornament of the London stage, whom she had known for eighteen years. They enjoyed a long working and emotional relationship, but whether it was a sexual one is unknown.

Ellen Terry as Portia in 1910.

Left: Henry Irving, one of the greatest actors of all time, in around 1896, when he started to come to Winchelsea as a frequent guest of Ellen Terry.

Below: Ellen Terry's Winchelsea home, Tower Cottage, with the Strand Gate beyond. (Terry Philpot)

Irving was separated but not divorced from his wife. The two actors holidayed together and exchanged long, affectionate letters. The year before she came to Winchelsea she began an extensive correspondence with George Bernard Shaw, which was at its most prolific until she moved from Tower Cottage.

Terry, always flamboyant and usually careless of convention, would go out in the early morning in the flimsiest of long white nightdresses and dance on the lawn in front of the house. When Joseph pulled her up on this, she laughed and said: 'Who's to see me, Joe, at five o'clock in the morning? There are only labourers going to work, and I don't mind amusing them. It's so good for the poor dears.'

Irving had read aloud to Terry and her daughter Edy and friends his preferred version of *Coriolanus*, which he had announced would open his 1896 season. They were unimpressed, thinking it dull. The next morning he called out to Terry from his bedroom that he wouldn't do it. 'Joy! Joy!' she exclaimed. But it was performed in 1901, and judged to be dull.

In 1900 Terry moved to Smallhythe Place, 10 miles to the north. She had seen it when driving in Kent with Irving and decided that she wanted to live and die there. That same year, when preparing to go with Irving on tour to the USA the following year, she asked her sister Kate if she could find a tenant for Winchelsea at £150 a year.

She died at Smallhythe Place, loved and adored, in 1928, having been on the stage for sixty-nine years.

Spike Milligan

Writer, actor, scriptwriter, comedian and goon, Spike Milligan moved to Carpenter's Meadows in Dumb Woman's Lane, Udimore, in 1986, with his third wife Shelagh Sinclair, whom he had married three years previously. The house cost £360,000 and was set in 3 acres, with five bedrooms, a tennis court and swimming pool, and 180-degree views from the cliffs above Hastings to Dungeness.

It was typical of Milligan's wish to shock and provoke that when asked on BBC's *Room 101* in 1999 to name his pet hates, he chose the house. He held up a picture of his home and said, 'It's bloody awful. When I saw a photograph, I said to the estate agent, "It looks as if it's made from white stone." He said, "Yes, it is." But it isn't. It's built from concrete blocks. It's all blank, blank, blank. That's why I hate it: because I own it.'

When the presenter, Paul Merton, asked what could be done to improve it, Milligan added thoughtfully, 'You could set fire to it.'

After his death, his wife said, 'It was the kind of thing he said. Actually, he grew very fond of the house. But when he said what he did on *Room 101* people believed him. And now I've got to sell it.'

They had moved from London where Milligan had become tired of being recognised. (When someone said 'You're Spike Milligan', he'd come back with, 'I know who I am. Now you go home and find out who you are.') The couple settled on Sussex because north of London was too far from Shelagh's family and he did not favour westward because of aircraft noise. She said, 'We both looked at each other and said, "We're not going east"'. Having been posted to Bexhill during the war, Milligan had a familiarity with the county, but he had gotten to know the Rye area because Peter Eton, the producer of *The Goon Show*, lived in Winchelsea, where Milligan visited him.

When the Milligans came to view what he would call 'the ugliest house in the world', his wife explained, 'Spike didn't say much when we came to look around. But he had always suffered from noise and his biggest concern was the seclusion and quiet. The rest didn't really come into the equation.'

There were touches of Milligan's humour around the house, in addition to his awards. In the downstairs toilet was a framed banknote from pre-revolutionary Russia, with a notice: 'In case of Restoration of Russian Monarchy Break Glass'. A picture frame in the kitchen read, 'Vegetarian – someone who is nice to meat'. On the mantelpiece a sign proclaimed, 'No smoking: we are trying to give up lung cancer'. Milligan was a campaigner against muzak, and in the hall was an award presented by the 'Right to Peace and Quiet Campaign'. The only change made to the house was the installation of a high-powered heater in the swimming pool which allowed Milligan to swim outdoors even on very cold days. Alas, too often fans called without invitation or announcement.

Milligan had a triple heart bypass operation in 1993, and he died of kidney failure aged eighty-three in 2002 at his home. Buried at Winchelsea, he signed off with a typical Milligan joke. His headstone is inscribed in Gaelic with the words 'I told them I was ill'.

In 2004 Shelagh put the house on the market for £800,000. In 2012 it sold for £1.6 million.

Spike Milligan's grave in St Thomas's churchyard, Rye. (Terry Philpot)

8. Keeping the Faith

St Mary's Church

St Mary's dates to the twelfth century, yet it boasts stained-glass windows created by Edward Burne-Jones and the Arts and Crafts pioneer William Morris, as well as a copy of the Geneva Bible. The first full edition appeared in 1560, and so preceded the King James' version by fifty-one years, making it the bible of Shakespeare, John Knox, and John Donne. This one is not dated but will likely have been later than 1616, when the last edition appeared.

Almost midway between the time of the original construction and when the windows were created the extraordinary clock was installed, made in 1561–62, with its two gilded cherubs with their striking bells above the face. The hours are struck and the quarters chime. The 18-foot pendulum, a later addition, can be seen in the body of the church. Above the clock face are the words from the Book of Wisdom: 'For our time is a very shadow that passeth away'.

The words above the sixteenth-century clock. (Paul Lantsbury)

Above: The bells of St Mary's.
(Paul Lantsbury)

Left: The Geneva Bible.
(Paul Lantsbury)

Revd Samuel Jeake

Samuel Jeake was involved in the two great controversies of his time: he was a Nonconformist preacher when it was dangerous to dissent from the practices of the Anglican Church, and he took the Parliamentary side during the Civil War.

He was born in 1623, the son of a baker and grandson of the Sussex minister John Pierson. His letters testify to a piety shared with his mother and her circle.

The joint letter to the Cromwellian general, Lord Fairfax, which Jeake orchestrated, saw victory for the Parliamentary side as a chance to initiate reform. Jeake's beliefs influenced his personal life: in the negotiations that preceded his marriage to Frances Hartridge in 1651, she submitted five 'propositions', one of which was her demand for 'libertie of conscience' in their marriage. Of their children, only one, Samuel, survived infancy.

Like many educated men of his day, Jeake was a polymath. In 1696 his son Samuel published posthumously his father's *Logistikēlogia, or, Arithmetick surveighed and reviewed.* Jeake was also interested in astrology and was a skilled calligrapher, which he may have practised professionally.

In 1651 he became town clerk of Rye, a post he held throughout the Commonwealth period, and from 1653 to 1656 he was also registrar for births, deaths and marriages.

With the restoration of the monarchy, he lost his job as town clerk, and in 1662, along with other supporters of the Parliamentary cause, he was disenfranchised. At this time he wrote, likely in 1678, *The Charters of the Cinque Ports*, which was published in 1728. He also remained as leader of Rye's Nonconformist congregation, which, it is believed, met in his house. As well as sermons, there remain many letters from his engagement in religious controversy, and others where he offered spiritual advice to his co-religionists.

Jeake practised as a lawyer in the 1660s and early 1670s and in 1682 one of his political opponents in the town described him as 'an amphibious creature between an attorney and a scrivener and has for many years been employed in most of the contracts and conveyances of the town and adjacent country'.

He amassed a great library, now long dispersed, that consisted of about 2,100 items, among which was a remarkable holding of the radical pamphlets of the Civil War and the Commonwealth period, together with learned works on subjects as varied as theology, literature, law, mathematics, science and magic.

Hartshorn House, as it looked in 1859 when it was subdivided, empty and in a poor state of repair. (Courtesy of Alan Dickinson)

One biographer comments: 'It is an outstanding example of a library of an unusual type, built up by a provincial, independent-minded book collector remote from the culture of church and university ... the catalogue ... provides a vivid record of its former glories.'

Jeake was not lacking in intellectual sustenance from others, divorced as the town might well be from that 'culture of church and university', for he spent time with John Allin, the vicar of Rye from 1653 to 1662, who stayed in touch through extensive correspondence after a move to London; Richard Hartshorn, the local schoolmaster, whose daughter was to marry Samuel Jr; and Philip Frith, a surgeon-apothecary, who was also a bibliophile and who, when he died in 1670, left his books to the younger Jeake, which were added to his father's library.

But despite his many interests and intellectual life, in the 1670s and 1680s Jeake's local prominence as a church leader made him an obvious target for persecution in Rye, as fellow Nonconformists who were persecuted elsewhere.

He was excommunicated in 1676, which did not dissuade him from defiantly facing Charles II in 1681, when the king replied to Jeake's invoking of the law by saying, 'If he were so much for Law, he should have it'. Jeake was prosecuted and his meeting was suppressed. The king's party gained such strength in the town that the next year Jeake fled to London, where wrote what has been described as 'an elaborate treatise on the chronology of the world from the creation to the flood'. At his death it was unfinished.

He came back to Rye in 1687 and took up again leadership of the local Nonconformists. It was suggested in August 1690 that he might resume the town clerkship with his son acting as his assistant. However, this was forestalled by illnesses that led to his death in October, having preached his last sermon two months before.

Revd John Allin

Suffolk-born John Allin was a notable dissenting clergyman, chemist and doctor in Rye but his main claim to historic significance is what happened when he was forced to leave the town due to the religious tests that came with the restoration of the Stuart monarchy in 1660. For his fleeing to London coincided with the Great (bubonic) Plague, which killed 100,000 Londoners in seven months.

His letters, describing the plague, were sent back to Rye, to friends like Revd Samuel Jeake, a fellow Nonconformist minister, and Philip Frith, local official and lay apothecary. Unlike the Black Death of 1346–53, when victims were buried in plague pits in Rye, the Great Plague affected mainly London and was only felt elsewhere when some people fled the city.

Allin reported to a friend in Rye:

I am through mercy yet well, in middest of death & that too approaching neerer & neerer: not many doores off, & the [burial] pitt open dayly within veiw [*sic*] of my chamber window, the Lord fitt mee & all of us for our last end.

At the end of the following month, addressing him as 'dear friend' and signing off as 'Your loving friend', he told Philip Frith:

I hope the lord will spare you to be useful to such as may want you in the land of the living. But we had need all be awakened to be ready, for we know not the day nor the hour when our lord will come, truly I think since the last bill the sickness is again encroaching and very much about us. I have hired my chamber again for another quarter of a year: if the lord grant life so long: I will if the lord please speedily collect my thoughts and finish this discourse of his sickness and send you, but I hinted in my last what a care and hurry I have been in...

Born in 1623 in Suffolk to John Allin (or Allen), also a clergyman, Allin was educated in Harvard, USA, when the family took themselves off to Massachusetts Bay Colony in 1637 in the face of the persecution of Puritan Nonconformists. Allin, like many contemporaries, was interested in alchemy and his interest may have begun in Harvard, for he shared rooms with George Starkey, who was well known for his alchemical work in London after 1651.

He used chemical experiments. Indeed, one historian, Donna Bilak, writes that Allin 'constitutes an important case study for understanding the realities of pre-modern alchemical practice, and its relationship with profound changes that emerged in medicine, natural philosophy, religion, and social life in the British Atlantic world.'

Before young Allin returned to England and to Rye, his mother died and his father married Catherine Dudley, widow of Thomas Dudley, governor of the colony, and one of their sons was the future colonial governor, Joseph Dudley, which gives Allin a step-relationship to colonial America's early government.

His coming to Rye coincided with the beginning of the Commonwealth and in 1649–50 he was one of 167 local citizens who declared loyalty to the new Lord Protector Oliver

Cromwell. He became a minister, married Hannah Smith, and became the father of three surviving children (his wife died with their stillborn son in 1661).

Allin was expelled from his parish when he refused to abide by the 1662 Act of Uniformity and while he stayed in the town until 1664, living we know not how, he was forced to leave for London that year. Bilak speculates that his enforced departure – leaving his children in the care of neighbours – may be connected to the death of William Hay, radical MP for Rye, who may have been Allin's political protector.

The letters largely form his extensive correspondence with Jeake and Frith. The three friends were millenarianists – promoters of the doctrine that a 1,000-year reign of blessedness will arrive, probably imminently, culminating in the second coming of Christ. For them the Book of Revelation foretold this and was betokened by the successful alchemical metallic transmutation.

Some of these letters are about medico-alchemical information. When in London, Allin facilitated the establishment of an alchemical laboratory in Rye for Frith and Jeake, and offered them guidance based on his own experiments in the capital.

He struck up various friendships in London, including with Spencer Pigott, first gardener at the Chelsea Physic Garden until he was dismissed in around 1677, and lived at various addresses. Refused a licence to practise medicine because of his Nonconformity, he offered medical services from his home. He was a member of a 'clubb of chimists', producing pharmaceuticals for both London and for shipping to Virginia.

In 1680 Allin went to America to become a minister in Woodbridge, New Jersey, where he died in 1683. He left no published work but there are 212 letters in the Sussex Record Office and an inventory drawn up in Woodbridge showed 380 books, comprising medico-alchemical, theological, mathematical, legal, and reference books, half of the inventory of his goods and possessions.

The Huguenots

Rye was well known as a stronghold of Protestantism – 'a godly commonwealth' it was said – even before the reign of Henry VIII and there was strong opposition to the imposition of the Mass in the reign of his daughter, Mary Tudor.

This, allied with the fact that it was a port and no great distance from France, made the town an obvious place of refuge for Huguenots, the French Protestants, who fled from their native country from the sixteenth to the eighteenth centuries. Rye and Winchelsea were the easiest places to reach from Dieppe. Huguenots had come to England at the time of the Tudors, especially under Edward and Elizabeth. By 1582 there were 1,500 people of French extraction living in Rye.

The two worst events that caused this refugee influx (the word 'refugee' has been bequeathed to us by these exiles) was, first, the massacre of 1,200 Protestant worshippers by Catholics at Vassy in 1562, and, second, the St Bartholomew's Day Massacre in Paris in 1572 when 30,000 Huguenots died, which set off other incidents of mass murder.

The Huguenots followed the teaching of John Calvin. Their situation had improved in France when in 1589, in the midst of one of the eight civil wars between 1562 and 1598 – the Wars of Religion – Henri de Bourbon, the Protestant king of Navarre, inherited the French throne. In 1593 he converted to Catholicism ('Paris is well worth a Mass').

When the civil wars ended five years later the now Henry IV proclaimed the Edict of Nantes, giving his former co-religious followers, who had fought with him, considerable privileges, which included a degree of religious tolerance.

The Rye Church, organised from the church in Threadneedle Street, London, in 1681, was conformist, in that it used the forms of worship of the Church of England, translated into French. (Many Huguenot churches resisted this but they still enjoyed a legal existence in England when English Dissenters did not.)

Bertrand, the minister in Rye, was, by his own admission, a little too Calvinist to favour Anglican tastes and preached on the 'happy deliverance from the ever-tyrannical yoke of the bishops'. His willingness to baptise children at home caused conformists offence.

Henry IV's grandson Louis XIV came to believe that a large religious minority was a threat to royal absolutism and the Huguenots' privileges were whittled away. In 1685 Louis published the Revocation of the Edict of Nantes, exiling the Protestant clergy but refusing the laity the right to leave the country.

But leave they did – eventually an estimated 200,000 of them – to more accepting places through Europe and as far as Russia, America and South Africa (where their descendants are among the Afrikaners). They tended to be professional and skilled people, often craftsmen like weavers or merchants. They were prominent in banking, commerce, industry, the book trade, the arts and the army.

Their legacy was to be a lasting one, from the opticians Dollond and Aitchison to the ancestors of the actors David Garrick and Laurence Olivier, and from the Houblon brothers who set up what became the Bank of England in 1694 to Peter Mark Roget and his thesaurus.

In 1685 fifty more families came to Rye. If those seeking to leave were caught, they were executed or sent as galley slaves on the French fleet. Women were imprisoned and their children sent to convents. Huguenot ministers officiated at St Mary's Church, where they were allotted specific times for their services.

Locally, their influence remains evident. For example, the clock of St Mary's – said to be one of the oldest turret clocks still working in the country – was made in 1561–62 by the Huguenot Lewys Billiard of Winchelsea.

The St Bartholomew's Day Massacre in 1572, one of the events that prompted Huguenots to flee France, as depicted by Frans Hogenberg.

William Jeaque (possibly Jacques) was a sixteenth-century merchant, the first of the family of that name (now Jeake) to settle in Rye. A bakery in the High Street was established by his son, Henry. Henry's son Samuel became town clerk under the Cromwellian Commonwealth, while his grandson, also Samuel, a wool merchant, built a storehouse that is now (after various uses) Jeake's House hotel.

The Huguenots were not without their blemishes: some, for example, took part in smuggling, while some residents resented them because they feared for their jobs.

The Promulgation of Tolerance to France's remaining Protestants was granted in 1787, with special rights to exiled Huguenot descendants to return. By then few did. Places like Rye and Winchelsea had welcomed them. They were now British.

The Methodists of Rye

In 1738 John Wesley, then an Anglican clergyman, was converted to the 'saving faith' he had sought, thus planting roots for what was to become the Methodist Church. He had first come to Rye in 1758 and only twenty-five years later, in 1773, Methodists had taken as a chapel an existing one next to what is now Hartshorn House in Mermaid Street. This property had been owned by Samuel Jeake Jr and after his death his widow, Elizabeth, was allowed to convert it to a Presbyterian chapel. Charles Wesley, the brother of John, preached there. When in 1789 the Methodists moved to a new chapel in Gun Garden, the building was taken over by the universalists and later demolished. In 1814 a larger Methodist church was built on the Gun Garden site but this was destroyed by bombing in the Second World War. The school opposite was converted to the present church and opened in 1954.

DID YOU KNOW?
Periteau House, High Street, Winchelsea, was named to commemorate a Huguenot resident whose family had fled to England to escape religious persecution in France.

Periteau House. (Terry Philpot)

Right: Revd John Wesley, who visited Rye and Winchelsea.

Below: The Methodist chapel, Winchelsea, where John Wesley preached.

St Augustine's unusual church tower. (Terry Philpot)

DID YOU KNOW?
St Augustine's Church, Brookland, Kent, is one of the country's most unusual-looking churches. Its bell tower, said to be made from the timber of local shipwrecks, is detached and sits next to the main structure of the church, like an upturned ice-cream cone.

Revd John Wesley comes to Winchelsea
John Wesley, the founder of Methodism, first came to Winchelsea from Rye in October 1771. The Methodists had originally congregated in houses or in the open air. Their first chapel was an old Presbyterian one that Samuel Jeake's widow built next to Hartshorn House or the Old Hospital (so-called because of its use for that purpose in Napoleonic times) opposite what is now Jeake's House Hotel in Mermaid Street, Rye, and here Wesley had preached to 'a considerable number of serious people'.

When in the area, he had stayed with the Holmans, at their home Cadborough House, Udimore Road, Rye. (That building was destroyed by bombing in the Second World War, but the present house, of similar design to its predecessor, was rebuilt on the same foundations.)

When Wesley came back to Winchelsea ('that poor skeleton of Ancient Winchelsea') in 1789, he could preach in Evens' Chapel, which was built in 1785. (Now the Methodist

The 'Wesley tree' in German Street, Winchelsea, grown from a sapling from the original, which came down in a storm in 1927 and under which John Wesley preached his last open-air sermon. (Terry Philpot)

chapel in Rectory Lane, it is little changed.) He was eighty-seven when he came back to preach on 7 October 1790.

Now the chapel was too small to hold the crowds so he had to preach in the open air, as he said, under 'a large tree' near the ruined church of St Thomas's Church, although he may have preached there before. (The ash tree, just outside the churchyard wall in German Street, grew from a cutting of the original, which was destroyed in a storm in 1927.)

'The Kingdom of Heaven is at hand. Repent and believe in the Gospel,' he urged the townspeople. 'It seems as if all that heard me were, at the present, almost persuaded to be Christian,' he said.

It was to be his last open-air sermon, fifty-one years after his first, for he died six months later.

The Roman altar in the Church of St Mary the Virgin, Stone in Oxney. (Leonard Bentley)

DID YOU KNOW?

The Church of St Mary the Virgin, Stone in Oxney, has what its guidebook describes as a stone Roman altar, 3 foot 4 inches high and almost square, with a basin hollowed out of the top and a bull set in relief at the base on all four sides. It is believed to be of Kentish ragstone quarried at Hythe and may have come from Stutfall Castle, the Roman fort at Lympne. The basin would have been for both libations offered to the god, believed to be Mithras, the soldiers' diety, and for animal sacrifice. Tradition has it that the altar was discovered under the floor of the north chapel, which raises the possibility that the church was built on a site of pagan worship, which was not uncommon. It remained in the church until the early eighteenth century when its pagan associations caused it to be removed and used as a horse block, which caused it to be damaged.

In 1753 the then incumbent Revd William Gosling rescued the stone and had it repaired and placed in the vicarage garden. In 1926 it was put back in the church. The Winchelsea writer John Saville had a theory that it was placed in the church as a symbol of Christianity's victory over Mithraism, a nice touch but without evidence.

Revd Alec Vidler

Alec Vidler was a Ryer by birth, a member of an old and respected town family made prosperous by its shipping business. In later life he not only came back to live in his native town, but he embarked on a new and very different career in local government, ending up as Rye borough's last mayor but also one who, at the time of his election, was not a member of the council.

Vidler was born in 1899 in the Old Stone House, Church Square, allegedly the only surviving part of a thirteenth-century priory of the Friars of the Sack (it may have been built by a local merchant), which his family had owned since 1801. He claimed that he was kissed in his pram by a neighbour, Henry James, who commented, 'What an intelligent-looking baby!' (In later life, Vidler became friendly with Burgess Noakes, who had been Henry James' manservant.) His father Leopold Amon Vidler, a local historian, raised £30,000 for the RNLI for the dependants and families of those who died in the lifeboat disaster of 1928. In 1934 Amon's *New History of Rye* was published.

Schooled in Kent, a short return to work in the family firm when his father was in the army (he himself served briefly as an officer cadet), and then Vidler was off to Cambridge to read theology, having felt the call to Anglican ordination. By 1923 he was a priest-companion in the small, celibate Anglo-Catholic Oratory of the Good Shepherd in Cambridge and he made a life profession in 1939.

Vidler served in various parishes, he electioneered for the Labour Party, and published, among other books, *Magic and Religion* (1930), *Sex, Marriage and Religion* (1932), *God's Judgement on Europe* (1940), and *Secular Despair and Christian Faith* (1941).

Despite his continuing membership of the Oratory, he moved away from High Anglicanism to theological liberalism. As warden of St Deiniol's Library, Hawarden, North Wales (now Gladstone's Library, it was created by the prime minister), he could spend more time writing, which included *A Plain Man's Guide to Christianity* (1936), as well as editing the magazine *Theology*. Well established as a Christian apologist, he was one of the great speakers at university missions.

When, in 1948, he became canon of St George's Chapel, Windsor, in the gift of George VI, he created his own unofficial theological college of middle-aged ordinands, called 'the Doves' or 'Vidler's vipers', according to one's inclination.

As dean of King's College, Cambridge, in 1958 he launched one of the most influential and intellectually heavyweight group of theologians of the post-war years. Vidler's television appearance added to his notoriety for unorthodox theology, and he also produced books challenging traditional understandings of Christianity.

When he retired in 1967 Vidler came back to live in the ancient house in which he had been born. He had avoided having what he called the 'noxious' device of the telephone in Cambridge but now had one in Rye that was ex-directory and only gave his number to those who needed it on the strict stipulation that they never passed it on.

Retired he may have been but he still lectured in the US and Europe and he took up painting, beekeeping, and writing pithy letters to *The Times*, as well as becoming the first chairman of the Rye Preservation Society. He also saw more of his lifelong friend (they had met at university) the writer and controversialist Malcolm Muggeridge, who lived in

The Old Stone House, Church Square, birthplace of Alec Vidler and his family home since 1801, to which he returned for a new career in local government later in life. (Paul Lantsbury)

nearby Robertsbridge. They met frequently for long walks and discussion and also made a television series on the journeys of St Paul.

Within six months of his return, Vidler was asked to stand for the council as a Ratepayers Association candidate, and won the seat, serving from 1968 to 1971. In 1972, although by then not on the council, he became the last mayor, after which the borough was absorbed into the new Rother District Council. His father, grandfather and great-grandfather had also held the post.

Alas, his ambition to die in the house in which he was born was not realised and he was living in a care home in Tenterden, Kent, when he died in 1991. He donated his body for medical research.

DID YOU KNOW?
During the Reformation, Jesuit priests took refuge in the Mermaid Inn, which dates back to 1156. Today the banned Jesuit symbol 'J.H.S.' can be seen carved into the oak panelling in 'Dr. Syn's Lounge' (the 'J' is reversed).

St Anthony of Padua Church
Rye's Catholic parish church, a small neo-Gothic church dedicated to St Walburga, was opened in 1900 on the present site in Watchbell Street.

The Church of St Anthony of Padua, opened in 1929. (Terry Philpot)

In 1910 the parish was handed over to the care of the Franciscan Friars, and by 1926 the congregation had outgrown St Walburga's. The architect John Bernard Mendham was commissioned to design a bigger church. He had been brought up in Buenos Aires and so was familiar with Spanish colonial architecture and mission churches and created his masterpiece in Rye.

It shows classical restrained decoration and is believed to be the only Spanish-Romanesque church in Britain. It was the first church built in England by the Franciscan Friars (officially the Order of Friars Minor Conventual of Britain and Ireland or the Greyfriars) since the days of Henry VIII.

Bibliography

I must thank the efficient and helpful staff of the British Library and the Society of Antiquaries, London, whose library possessed a book that, uniquely in my experience, was not in the British Library's stock (Martin *et al*). Again, the *Oxford Dictionary of National Biography* proved to be indispensible.

In writing this book, I have read or consulted the following books and publications:

Ackland, Michael, *Henry Handel Richardson. A Life* (Cambridge: Cambridge University Press, 2004)

Aiken, Joan*, The Haunting of Lamb House* (London: Jonathan Cape, 1991)

Arnold, David, 'Winchelsea, terrible tempests and laughing frogs', *Hastings & St Leonard's Observer*, 3 February 2017

Batsford, Cook, Brian, *The Britain of Brian Cook* (London: B T Batsford, 1987)

Batsford Cook, Brian, *Brian Cook's Landscapes of Britain* (London: Batsford, 2010)

Benson, E. F., *More Spook Stories* (London: Hutchinson, 1934)

Benson, E.F., *The Collected Ghost Stories*, edited by Richard Dalby (London: Robinson Publishing: 1992)

Bilak, Donna, *The Chymical Cleric: John Allin, Puritan Alchemist in England and America (1623–1683)* (New York: The Bard Graduate Centre, 2013, PhD dissertation)

Blomfield, Reginald, *Memoirs of an Architect* (London: Macmillan and Co., 1932)

Brentnall, Margaret, *The Cinque Ports and Romney Marsh* (London: John Gifford, 2nd edition, 1980)

Channer, Nick, *Writers' Houses: Where Great Books Began* (London: Robert Hale, 2015)

Chisholm, Anne, *Rumer Godden: A Storyteller's Life* (London: Macmillan, 1998)

Clark, Ross, 'The ugliest house in the world', *Daily Telegraph*, 28 April 2004

Corcoran, Desmond, 'A Rye View', *Tate Etc*, 1 January 2008

Delbanco, Nicholas, *Group Portrait: Joseph Conrad, Stephen Crane, Ford Madox Ford, Henry James and H. G. Wells* (London, Faber & Faber, 1882)

Dickinson, Alan, with Foster, Heidi, and Dickinson, Oliver, *Rye Though Time* (Stroud: Amberley Publishing, 2011)

Dickinson, Alan, *Rye and Around in Old Photographs* (Stroud: Amberley Publishing, 2016)

Dickinson, Patric, *Poems from Rye* (Rye: Martello Bookshop, 1979).

Dimmock, Matthew, Hadfield, Andrew and Quinn, Paul (eds), *Art, Literature and Religion in Early Modern Sussex: Culture and Conflict* (Farnham, Surrey: Ashgate, 2014)

Draper, Gillian, *Rye: A History of a Sussex Cinque Port to 1660* (Chichester: Phillimore, 2009)

Dunan-Page, Anne, *The Religious Culture and the Huguenots 1660–1750* (Aldershot: Ashgate, 2006)

Eates, Margot, *Paul Nash: Master of the Image, 1889–1946* (London: John Murray, 1973)

Edel, Leon, *Henry James: A Life* (London: William Collins Sons and Company, 1985)

Fellows, Richard, A., *Sir Reginald Blomfield: An Edwardian Architect* (London: A. Zwemmer, 1985)

Findlayson, Ian, *Writers in Romney Marsh* (London: Severn House Publishers, 1986)

Foord, Keith, D., *Winchelsea Historic Methodist Chapel* (Battle: Battle Methodist Church, 2013)

Friends of Rye Harbour, *Rye Harbour* (Rye: Rye Harbour Nature Reserve, no date)

Greeves, Lydia, *Houses of the National Trust* (London: National Trust Books, 2008)

Gregory, Annabel, *Rye Spirits: Faith, Faction and Fairies in a Seventeen Century English Town* (London: The Hedge Press, 2013)

Gregory, Annabel, 'The true face of witchcraft', *History Today*, August 2016

Hyde, H. Montgomery, *Henry James at Home* (London, Methuen & Co., 1969)

James, Henry, 'An English Winter Watering Place', in *Collected Travel Writings: Great Britain and America* (New York: Library of America, 1993)

Leslie, Anita, *Cousin Clare: The Tempestuous Career of Clare Sheridan* (London: Hutchinson & Co., 1976)

Locke, Tim, *Slow Sussex and South Downs Natural Park* (Chalfont St Peter: Bradt, 2011)

Mackenzie, Eileen, *The Findlater Sisters. Literature & Friendship* (London: John Murray, 1964)

Manvell, Roger, *Ellen Terry* (London: William Heinemann, 1968)

Martin, David, Martin and Barbara, with Clubb, Jane, and Draper, Gillian, *Rye Rebuilt. Regeneration and Decline within a Sussex Port Town 1350–1660* (Burgess Hill: Domtom Publishing, 2009)

Melville, Joy, *Ellen Terry* (London: Haus Publishing, 2006)

Monod, Paul Kléber, *The Murder of Mr Grebell. Madness and Civility in an English Town* (London and Yale: Yale University Press, 2003)

O'Hanlon, Mark, *Beyond the Lonely Pine: A Biography of Malcolm Saville* (Worcester: Mark O'Hanlon, 2001)

Palmer, Geoffrey, and Lloyd, Noel, *E. F. Benson as He Was* (Luton: Lennard Publishing, 1988)

Platt, Richard, *Smuggling in the British Isles: A History* (Stroud: Tempus Publishing, 2007)

Priest, Christopher, 'John Christopher', *The Guardian*, 6 February 2012

Reavell, Cynthia and Tony, *E. F. Benson: Mr Benson Remembered in Rye and the World of Tilling* (Rye: Martello Bookshop, 1984)

Saville, Malcolm, *Portrait of Rye* (East Grinstead: Henry Goulden, 1976)

Seymour, Miranda, *A Ring of Conspirators: Henry James and His Literary Circle 1895–1915* (London: Scribner, 2004)

Souhami, Diana, *The Trials of Radclyffe Hall* (London: Quercus, new edition, 2013)

Stevenson, Jane, *Edward Burra: Twentieth Century Eye* (London: Pimlico, 2008)

Taylor, Betty, *Clare Sheridan* (Hastings: Hastings Press, 2007)

Taylor, Rupert, *The East Sussex Countryside Book* (Newbury: Countryside Books, 1999)

Thorpe, Laura, 'The Great Plaque of 1665: Case Closed?', *History Today*, 9 September 2016

Toibin, Colm, *The Master* (London: Picador, 2004)

Vidler, Alec R., *Scenes from a Clerical Life* (London: Collins, 1977)

Wright, Norman, *The Famous Five: Everything You Wanted to Know* (London: Hodder Children's Books, 2004)

Yeandle, W. H., *Historical Notes on the Church of Stone-in-Oxney* (1934. Out of print but available on the church's website, www.stoneinoxneychurch.org)

Acknowledgements

I am grateful to the following people for their help:

In the absence of any very recently available information about Brede Place, Lesley Bannister, clerk to the Brede Parish Council, kindly informed me that it is now a private residence. Victoria Bevan, curator of Lamb House, was helpful regarding the date of the property's construction in the face of several conflicting dates. Martin Blincow, guest relations manager at the Mermaid Inn, supplied information regarding the known and alleged tunnels in the hotel. Rosemary Burt, Rother District Council's cemetery officer, helped me regarding Rye Cemetery. Allan Downend, secretary of the E. F. Benson Society, clarified the often confusing statements about E. F. Benson's tenancy of Lamb House. Clarification, too, came from Jo Kirkham, chairman of the Rye Museum, regarding the history of the site on which the present Rye, Winchelsea and District Memorial Hospital is built, as well as information about the sites of early Methodist meeting places in Rye. Keith Foord, historian of Sussex Methodism, kindly read a draft of the entry on John Wesley. I spent an enjoyable day with Paul Lantsbury, who took the photographs attributed to him. Alex May, senior editor of the *Oxford Dictionary of National Biography*, offered evidence, in the face of conflicting statements, about where Edward Burra was born (London). Professor Paul Kléber Monod helped me understand better the confusion of minimal fact and maximum fantasy that he so masterfully unpicks in his book *The Murder of Mr. Grebell: Madness and Civility in an English Town*. Mark O'Hanlon, founder of the Malcolm Saville Society, gave me information about when Saville lived in Winchelsea, and also led me to his excellent biography of Saville, *Beyond the Lone Pine*. Jane Stevenson, author of the definitive life of Edward Burra, kindly sent me a genealogy of the Burra family, which she had constructed. Last, I have to thank Alan Murphy, commissioning editor at Amberley Publishing, and his colleagues, who, from commission to final production, brought this book to life.